Praise for *The Jaws Log*

"*The Jaws Log* is to this day my favorite piece of 'making-of' material. It's like a little movie director bible. Whenever I'm having a bad day at work, I go back and read a chapter…and thank the Lord I'm not shooting on the ocean."

—**BRYAN SINGER**, Director, *The Usual Suspects, X-Men*

"*Jaws* is one of those movies where the 'making-of' story is nearly as good as the movie itself, especially when it is told by the unsung hero of that story, the screenwriter. Because above and beyond the Spielberg touch and the fine acting, the reason *Jaws* is a great, great movie is the script, with its juicy characters. Carl Gottlieb wrote that script, and his behind-the-scenes account of the production is riveting."

—**PETER BISKIND**, Author, *Easy Riders, Raging Bulls*

"It's an easy read, energizing and with some of the zest of the movie—which is, of course, the funniest scare picture ever made." —**PAULINE KAEL**, Film Critic and Author

"Like Jonah writing from the belly of the whale, Carl Gottlieb's journal of the process of making *Jaws* comes from the unique perspective of one of the major players in the collaboration that resulted in Spielberg's classic movie."

—**JOHN LANDIS**, Director, *The Blues Brothers*

"Since *The Jaws Log* was first published, we've seen countless behind-the-scenes accounts of the making of movies, but none come close to Carl Gottlieb's artful, detailed, and very funny account of the making of this motion picture phenomenon. It is not only entertaining and insightful, but truly enhances one's appreciation of a remarkable filmmaker's achievement." —**ROB REINER**, Director,
A Few Good Men, When Harry Met Sally

"All of my life, I have been a devotee of film literature. Carl Gottlieb's *The Jaws Log* stands firmly at the top, easily the greatest 'making-of' book ever written, with its combination of humor, insight, and suspense of a production gone haywire. Gottlieb's work is as entertaining as the movie it is about. In fact, you have not had the full *Jaws* experience until you have read, make that *devoured*, this wonderful book."

—ROD LURIE, Director, *The Contender*,
Former President, Broadcast Film Critics Assn.

"For me, re-reading Carl's book was more than merely pleasurable. I'd forgotten how rich it is in detail about the movie business in general and about the appalling odds and apparently insurmountable obstacles...At the end of his afterword to this new addition, while acknowledging the subjectivity and fallibility of memory, Carl says of his story, 'This was how I saw it.' Well, as far as I'm concerned, this is how it *was*."

—PETER BENCHLEY, Author of *Jaws*, from his foreword

"No, *The Jaws Log* is not a candy bar. It's a wonderful book about a classic movie."

—STEVE MARTIN, actor, director, and author

"Steven Soderbergh has been like this ever since he saw *Jaws* and became obsessed, seeing it again and again, and reading and rereading *The Jaws Log* by Carl Gottlieb, highlighting things in it and going through several copies, wearing them out."   —*Rolling Stone*

The
Jaws
Log

25th Anniversary Edition

CARL GOTTLIEB

with an Introduction by Peter Benchley
and New Endnotes by Carl Gottlieb

NEWMARKET PRESS • NEW YORK

10 9 8 7 6 5 4 3 2 1

Library of Congress Cataloging-in-Publication Data
Gottlieb, Carl.
The Jaws log / Carl Gottlieb. — 2nd ed. / [introduction by Peter Benchley].
p. cm. — (A Newmarket insider filmbook)
"25th anniversary edition"—Cover.
Previous ed. published: New York : Dell, ©1975
ISBN 1-55704-458-9 (pbk. : alk. paper)
1. Jaws (Motion picture) I. Title. II. Series.
PN1997.J343 G68   2001
791.43'72—dc21   2001030309

Quantity Purchases
Companies, professional groups, clubs, and other organizations may qualify
for special terms when ordering quantities of this title. For information, write
Special Sales, Newmarket Press, 18 East 48th Street, New York, NY 10017,
call (212) 832-3575, fax (212) 832-3629, or e-mail mailbox@newmarketpress.com

www.newmarketpress.com

Manufactured in the United States of America

*To friends and fans
for their help, their endurance,
their enthusiasm, and their forbearance*

Table of Contents

Introduction

Peter Benchley

When I agreed to write these few words as a preface to the new edition of *The Jaws Log*, I saw no need to re-read the whole book. I recalled reading it in 1975 and thinking then that it was an admirably accurate, balanced, and fair account of the making of the movie.

Furthermore, over the ensuing twenty-five years, I had become comfortable with the recollections my personal memory bank had selected and shaped, and I wasn't interested in disturbing the peace.

I opened the book, prepared to skim through it—just for refreshment, you understand—and was hooked. Instantly. I couldn't put it down till I had read it straight through to the endnotes and final credits, for I found myself awash in vivid memories of the most astonishing, tumultuous, and momentous months of my life. Back in 1973 and 1974, nobody —myself least of all—knew that we were involved in the birth of a phenomenon that would retain a strange resonance in the culture for a *quarter of a century* . . . and in the worldwide debut of a director who would go on to influence the film industry like none other.

All of us, however, knew that we were witnessing something memorable, exciting, probably unprecedented, and, at times, altogether weird.

The making of *Jaws* has been chronicled *ad nauseam*, in print, on film, audio tape, video tape, laserdisc, and, most recently, DVD. But no one in any medium has come close to being as comprehensive or, more important, as accurate as Carl Gottlieb is in his updated *Jaws Log*. (In sheer, raw volume, of course, the Internet overwhelms everyone, but it's unreliable: too many so-called facts go out into cyberspace unchecked and, often, dead wrong. I'm misquoted in the digital ether all the time, often credited with quips and epigrams that were actually uttered by my grandfather, who died in 1945.)

For me, re-reading Carl's book was more than merely pleasurable. I'd forgotten how rich it is in detail about the movie business in general and about the appalling odds and apparently insurmountable obstacles that faced the brave souls determined to make *Jaws* on the open sea. I came away with renewed respect—"awe" is probably a better word—for the then twenty-six-year-old Steven Spielberg; for Director of Photography Bill Butler; for the incomparable producers, Richard Zanuck and David Brown; for the late and beloved Verna Fields; for Carl Gottlieb himself . . . and for many of the other characters you'll meet here.

At the end of his foreword, while acknowledging the subjectivity and fallibility of memory, Carl says of his story, "This was how I saw it."

Well, as far as I'm concerned, this is how it *was*.

Foreword

When the film was made and this book first written, *Jaws* was not yet a show business phenomenon and pop culture icon. It's axiomatic in the entertainment industry that no one can tell in advance and with any degree of certainty what constitutes a hit. In an era of mass marketing, product testing, audience research, and $20 million opening-weekend media buys, we still can't tell the audience what they like. When the last ticket's sold and the last kernel of popcorn is swept up, they tell us.

On the macro-economic scale, *Jaws* made film history as the highest-grossing movie of all time, and established a business model and release pattern for large-scale summer movies that persists to this day. On the micro-esthetic scale, it was one of the happiest collaborations of my career. Steven Spielberg's innate and preternatural talent for understanding audiences and his genius for making movies was not yet common knowledge; we had him to ourselves before he was a global resource. I only regret that memory is an overcrowded storage medium that loses crucial information and recollects personal experience imperfectly at best. I'm in my anecdotage, and I can't entirely remember how much fun I've had. What remains available still gives me pleasure to recall and enjoyment to relate.

Failure is an orphan, success has many parents. Over the years, *Jaws* has attracted fanatic fans, fierce critics, and more than its share of rumor and conjecture. Journalists recycle old and inaccurate material, participants suffer from selective memories, and almost everyone connected with the picture has been interviewed, photographed, consulted, recorded, and featured in documentaries, official and unofficial. The information available is still fragmentary and occasionally contradictory.

When I collaborated with David Crosby on his autobiography, my research into his personal history would occasionally conflict with his memory of events. Most of the time, he'd graciously concede that a preponderance of the evidence supported an alternative view of how things happened. A few times, he'd bark, "It's my life, and I'll remember it the way I want to." That's how the text of that book (and this one) were finally written.

Jaws was my life in 1975, and I remember it the way I want to, because I worked directly from my hand-scribbled notes, based on live interviews with the players who were there, as I was. The text reflects the reality that existed then. Movies, like most art forms, embrace a heightened reality. Creating or revising a screenplay, freedom is absolute. I'm free to drop or combine characters, change their age, sex, individuality, personal history, motivation, the circumstances of their birth, the manner of their death. The narrative is flexible, events are arbitrary, and the writer dictates the weather, the flavor of food, the size of the fish, the age of the wine. Or not, depending on budget, time, which sets are already built, which actors are cast, what the director wants to shoot, what the producers and studio think they want to see, and what's actually out there when the cameras finally roll.

Real life is far less organized than movies. In Fort Leonard Wood, Missouri, my old sergeant used to warn us troops about the perils of civilian life: "There's two hundred million people out there just walkin' around," he'd say ruefully. "And there ain't nobody in charge." Writing nonfiction is like that—it carries an obligation to some sort of objective reality, however imperfectly perceived. There are a lot of facts out there with no one in charge. Therefore, I've left the original narrative intact, except for minor spelling changes and a few stylistic fixes.

Which is not to say that I haven't learned anything since 1975. Twenty-five years is enough time for retrospection and receiving new information, so I've added endnotes to the text throughout. These are updates, factual corrections, and personal asides motivated by candor, pique, and impulse. The endnotes are intended to bring the reader up to date on the whereabouts and circumstances of key members of the cast and crew. In this regard, the World Wide Web was my most complete source of talent credits. I'm thankful for the Internet Movie Database (www.imbd.com), for its comprehensive and generally accurate list of credits. I can recommend it to anyone who wants to know everything about the people who made *Jaws*: the above-the-line talent (writers, director, producers, and actors) and key below-the-line personnel (production managers, assistant directors, cinematographers and camera persons, production designer, etc.). I'm also grateful to members of the online community for their interest, and for putting up and maintaining the many unofficial Web sites dedicated to *Jaws* and its sequels; many of them are listed in the endnotes. You guys are amazing!

To the crew that supplied immeasurable assistance, support, and encouragement in the writing and production of this edition, I'd also like to express my deepest appreciation: Marcia Jacobs, Kelli Maroney, Alex Simon, and Allison Caine Gottlieb, who was there then, and was of great help this time around. My cousin Paul Gottlieb, a publisher himself, always believed in this book and urged me to retrieve the rights. In the end, he acted as my agent and actually sold the project, so he's earned every penny of his commission, as well as my many, many thanks.

I am also beholden to Esther Margolis, a patient and talented publisher, for this edition. Her company, Newmarket Press, is an invaluable resource, both for authors and for audiences interested in movies. Keith Hollaman edited the new edition happily and well, and Nancy Cushing-Jones, Bette Einbinder, and Thomas Meissnest at Universal facilitated the use of Lewis Goldman's photos.

Everyone remembers things his or her own way, and suggestion and repetition inevitably affect recollection. If some people can confidently express false memories of ritual satanic abuse, the cast and crew and witnesses to *Jaws* can certainly disagree as to who did what and with which and to whom during the summer of 1974 in Martha's Vineyard and Hollywood.

This was how I saw it.

Carl Gottlieb
Hollywood, 2000

CHAPTER ONE

"Some Introductions Are in Order."

(June 1971–December 1972)

The shark can locate its prey several ways: he can smell blood from miles away, and he can sense vibrations in the water (as Peter Benchley points out in *Jaws*):

> A hundred yards offshore, the fish sensed a change in the sea's rhythm . . . running within the length of its body were a series of thin canals, filled with mucus and dotted with nerve endings, and these nerves detected vibrations and signaled the brain . . .

—*Jaws*, Chapter 1

Richard Zanuck and David Brown are Hollywood producers; although not filled with mucus, they are certainly dotted with nerve endings, and just as the great white shark can sense erratic vibrations of a swimmer in the water, so can Richard and David sense the movement of a literary property in the publishing world. They are not sharks, and they are not predators, but they are sensitive, and *Jaws* was still an unpublished manuscript at Doubleday when the vibrations created by its progress signaled the Zanuck/Brown Company that Something Was Up.

Both men have explained to me that they have private sources in the publishing world, and they are not alone in this. Studios and producers are always on the lookout for a marketable property, a book or story that appears attractive enough to justify the expense of transforming it into a film script, and popular enough to justify the further colossal expense of making it into a theatrical feature film where $100 million are at stake, and where the intense collaborative process of creation can occupy months, or years, before a finished film can be released.

Be assured that whenever you read a work of popular fiction or light storytelling, it has been studied and analyzed by a number of people who are professionals at the acquisition of literary properties. If you say to yourself, "This would be a terrific movie," chances are it may be, or at least someone has bought the rights to try and make it so.

Publishers routinely send copies of books while still in prepublication galley proof form to studios and major producers, looking for a movie sale, because they share in the proceeds of those sales. That's why when you buy a popular paperback, it frequently has the additional exhortation (or warning) "Soon to Be a Major Motion Picture." Many of these become Minor Motion Pictures, and still others become no motion picture at all, because someone guessed wrong, and the property became unpackageable, meaning that no "important" stars or directors or screen adapters would commit their services to the story within the time needed to make it.[1]

Jaws all began in June 1971, when Peter Benchley delivered a four-page outline of a proposed novel to an interested editor at the New York publishing house of Doubleday. Peter's pages and a favorable editor's memo were circulated in-house, and enough editorial support was gathered to justify the issuance of a contract request for Peter; that request was approved by a publishing board, and after a little stiff negotiating, the contract was approved and entered into by both parties. The contract, according to *The New York Times,* called for delivery of the first four chapters by April 15, 1972. It also called for a payment of $1,000 to Peter for his efforts, and the promise of a regular, larger advance if Doubleday decided to go ahead and do the whole book.

After revisions, rewrites, deadlines, and rewrites, Peter's book was finished and the final draft delivered in January 1973. During this period of internal preparation, the book about a shark got its title, *Jaws,* and a release date (autumn), as well as a massive assist in the form of a paperback book sale.

At this point, Peter, for having written a whole novel, had received a $7,500 advance; this for a year's work and a lifetime's preparation. Not only was it less than he was used to making as a professional writer, it was spread out over a lengthy period: $1,000 for the option on the first four chapters (already paid), $2,500 on the signing of the contracts. That gave Peter $3,500 to live on while he wrote the novel. The next $2,000 would be paid when he delivered the first draft, and then, after revisions, which could theoretically take a year or so, he would get the final $2,000. So far, not a big deal.[2]

When the novel had been finished, on the day the paperback sale was closed, Peter Benchley had $600 left in his bank account and had been out of work eight weeks, which is a long time when you're used to a steady paycheck. He was about to ask for a job on the *National Geographic,* and that's the truth.

Now, as far as I can determine, in the world of publishing, the paperback publisher is like the tooth fairy. The child (author) writes a novel or something. His parent (hardcover publisher) subsidizes the work, hoping that the kid will make something out of himself, and that enough people will buy the thing to take care of the publisher in his old age, or at least make him able to afford to have other kids, some of whom are bound to be retarded or worse, due to some genetic defect in the publisher's line.

Anyway, when the kid loses his tooth (the manuscript), the parent advises him to place it under the pillow, and to wait for the tooth fairy. Meanwhile, the parent/publisher tries to interest a paperback publisher to come up with some additional bucks for the kid, in which the parent will share.

In the case of Doubleday and Peter Benchley, the tooth fairy came through like a champ. After careful internal hype and the subsequently spirited bidding, a deal was consummated in which Bantam paid $575,000 for the paperback rights. Bonanza! The book clubs came through with their end of more deals, and suddenly *Jaws* was a major property, besides being an eminently entertaining novel. The publication date was moved back to allow a carefully orchestrated release of the book, first in hardcover and then in the book clubs, after which the paperback guys would move in with their national campaign, designed to sell books by the millions in mass distribution.

In the case of *Jaws*, the advance word was a vibration in the water. There was some internal hype at the publisher's— after all, the sales force had to be encouraged to get behind the book and push it to the booksellers. There was some talk among shark people, professionals like Peter Gimbel, who had produced the successful and scary documentary *Blue Water, White Death*, also about the great white shark. Through their own grapevine, they had heard that Peter Benchley (who dives and writes about the sea) was into a novel about sharks. This, in itself, must have been interesting gossip—if you were a CPA, and someone, somewhere, did the definitive accounts receivable novel, don't you think there'd be talk down at the CPA lodge hall?

Anyway, that's how the vibrations started, and Richard and David, like sensitive sharks, began to swim quietly and purposefully toward the source. Now sharks have been known to injure and kill themselves attacking boat pro-pellers, which are also a source of vibrations, and Dick and Dave have been swimming around Hollywood too long to bust their snouts on something as fixed and unappetizing as the twin screws on a marine diesel somewhere, so they circled, and waited until the big splash. In this case, it was the paperback sale. This was a big enough vibration to warrant serious attention, and the game was on.

CHAPTER TWO

"How a Book Becomes a Movie, Part One."

(January–May 1973)

Richard Zanuck and David Brown are an interesting team, a brace of gentlemen with clearly divided and resolutely assumed areas of responsibility. Dick is second-generation Hollywood mogul, the son of the more-or-less legendary Darryl F. Zanuck, and both father and son have played pivotal and essential roles in the history of the film community in general, and in the affairs of Twentieth Century Fox studios in particular.

When Dick Zanuck was head of production at Fox, he had gotten the job from his father, who had been named president of the company after a bitter proxy fight that is part of Hollywood legend. That his father fired him from the studio is yet another Tinseltown classic. Dick had been brought up to head production at Fox, working since student days as a laborer, in the editing rooms, and in the advertising department. He was born and brought up knowing the picture business from the bottom and the inside, and like any shoemaker's son, apprenticed to learn his father's trade. Just as I would want a second-generation mechanic to fix my car or a shoemaker's son to replace the heels on my shoes, so would I want a second-generation studio head to produce my picture.

It's my considered opinion that Richard Zanuck knows as much about the business of making movies as anyone alive today, and more than most any other executive currently heading a major studio or distributorship. He and David are responsible for a long string of popular and entertaining films that include Fox hits like *The Sound of Music, The French Connection, Patton,* and *Butch Cassidy and the Sundance Kid,* and when they moved to Universal, they gave that studio its first Best Picture Oscar in forty-five years with *The Sting,* on which they served as executive producers.

In addition to his production duties, David Brown is the "literary" half of the Zanuck/Brown team. He's based in New York, with his wife, Helen Gurley Brown, the highly successful editor of *Cosmopolitan.* From this vantage David can keep a close ear and eye turned to the publishing world. He is a former newspaperman and journalist (he was a managing editor of *Cosmopolitan* once), and like Zanuck, he is a graduate of Stanford University (only a decade or so earlier) and of the Hollywood studio world.[3]

Publishing is one of the few remaining public arts left on the East Coast, along with advertising, and, by self-definition, "Broadway."[4] But David Brown reads a lot, listens a lot, and always speaks with quiet elegance and precision. He's taller than Richard Zanuck, but seemingly less competitive. Both are articulate when they discuss the picture business; when they work together, the meshing of their individual talents becomes a wondrous blend of ability, insight, and experience. They know how and when to spend money on a picture, and I can ruefully assure you that they know exactly where they can cut a few dollars.[5]

One of the Zanuck/Brown hallmarks is their ability to move fast once they are interested in something. Their phones are manned by efficient secretaries, their locations are always known, and they have access—access to galley proofs, to publishers' information, to agents and lawyers. Who's not going to be in to the producers who paid $400,000 for the original screenplay of *Butch Cassidy and the Sundance Kid*, the guys who made *The Sting* one of the all-time top-grossing attractions and Oscar winners? So, once they became interested, it became a matter of negotiation.

There is something heady about big-money film deals, and just as sharks throw themselves into a feeding frenzy over a horse haunch thrown over the side, so did the agents involved in *Jaws* start swimming in circles and snapping at each other. There was Roberta Pryor, Peter's agent in the New York office of International Famous Artists (I.F.A.), the large agency since merged with Creative Management Associates (C.M.A.) to form International Creative Management (I.C.M.). In the California office there were John Ptak and Mike Medavoy, specialists in film negotiations and packaging. (Medavoy had been at C.M.A., which he left to go to I.F.A., which he left to become a production head at United Artists, where he could assemble projects for actual production, instead of packaging projects for actual sale.)

There were agents on both coasts, and so were Zanuck and Brown: Richard was handling the negotiations in L.A., while David did the talking to the New York people. At one point, both principals were seated in different chic restaurants in New York and Los Angeles—Dick at The Bistro in Beverly Hills, and David at The Palm in New York. They were both negotiating for the book with different agents, and such is their teamwork that they excused themselves and called each other from pay phones to confirm with each other that they were both making substantially the same offers. The agents sitting in the booths had to wait to get home to call and find out how they were doing, and I'm sure the executive slip-away-and-call paid off in the finally settled price for the film rights to the book.

So, they moved fast, and hard. Not as fast and hard as they did when they bought *Butch Cassidy* for Fox, but at that time Dick's authority as production head was limited in his contract to $200,000, and when he and David were through bidding and had closed the deal, it was past midnight and they were personally liable for the other $200,000 of the purchase price. I imagine that they and Fox fixed their personal liability so that it wouldn't actually be coming out of their pockets when the office opened in the morning, but, in the meantime, they had committed their lives, their fortunes, and their sacred honor to $400,000 for a William Goldman original screenplay.

In the months to come, there would surely have been other, bigger dollar offers for *Jaws*, but at this early stage, Richard and David had concluded their deal and now owned the rights to make the film of what might (or might not) be a best-seller. Remember, the book was still in galleys, and copies had not even been printed yet, much less put in Brentano's and Walden's windows and sold.[6]

I suppose you can attribute their success in acquiring this particular book to several factors: their willingness to talk big money early, the assurance that any project they put together would receive favorable consideration from Universal Studios where they hang their production hats, their own not inconsiderable charm as gentlemen, and their proven track record in the past. In addition, they assured Peter's agents that the film would be a personal production of theirs. (In this it would differ from *The Sting*, where Dick and David served as executive producers, and Michael and Julia Phillips and Tony Bill served as line producers. The difference is an executive producer finds the deal and supervises the construction of the package, whereas the line producer has to actually make the picture. What Dick and David had promised was that they would themselves attend to all the myriad details that are involved in the production of a major feature picture. Another difference is that it was the line producers of *The Sting* who went up to claim the little bronze statues at the annual presentation ceremonies of the Academy of Motion Picture Arts and Sciences.)

The deal was closed for a base price of $150,000, plus $25,000 for Peter to write the first draft of the screenplay.

With various escalations, the eventual price tag might have been as high as $250,000, which would not only include the rights to the book, but also a screenplay and two sets of revisions by the book's author. So far, so good.

CHAPTER THREE

"How a Book Becomes a Movie, Part Two."

(May–December 1973)

By now, with the film rights safely sewn up, it's time to take the package seriously. The Zanuck/Brown Company is an independent production unit with tight contractual ties to Universal Studios. Essentially, this means they have offices on the Universal lot, and that the properties they acquire will be Universal productions, with a complicated formula for division of profits and risks. In any event, *Jaws*, being a Zanuck/Brown Production, would also be a Universal picture. Universal is the last of the giant film factories, the only studio that still operates the way studios used to, before television and antitrust decrees and changing audience patterns broke them and made them into hollow shells of their former gaudy façades. Nowadays the studios are no longer run by executives who had their roots in production and exhibition, and autocratic bosses are giving way to corporate conglomerates with divided responsibilities. Universal Studios, however, has a tradition of being run by a firm and knowledgeable hand connected to a business brain of the first magnitude, with the unique Hollywood distinction that the hand and the brain belonged to the same man—Lew Wasserman, now chairman of the board of MCA. The

27

executive who headed television production at the studio for years, Sid Sheinberg, is now president of MCA, the corporate structure that controls Universal, following Wasserman as the second man in charge since MCA acquired Universal in 1959. So, with a history of one-man rule and profitable quarters, Universal has a vested interest in continuing operations in its own studio way.[7]

What this means, to the average producer working on the lot, is that the studio is going to charge a whopping overhead onto the budget for any picture, giving in return the services of the entire studio organization, with all its knowledgeable department heads, construction engineers, scenic artists, and so on down the line to the man who drives the mobile dressing rooms and toilets; modern, well-appointed facilities manufactured by a subsidiary of MCA, Inc.

It also means that, as in any large organization, there is bound to be a certain amount of deadwood and departmental boondoggling, and a tendency to do things the same way each time—"It worked on *Airport*, why won't it work on *Jaws?*" as well as, "Why not use Victoria Principal? She's under contract here and she owes us a picture." You can't actually blame anyone for anything, but there is a certain approach to studio picture-making that tends to make what should be serious aesthetic choices on the basis of past experience, good or bad, on exigencies of distribution and scheduling that have nothing to do with the individual project at hand. Granted, it's getting better all the time, but Universal is a big operation, and in big operations, things get better slower.

In the case of *Jaws*, and Zanuck and Brown, Universal was a trifle wary. True, *The Sting* had grossed more than $100 million worldwide, and a multimillion-dollar gross covers a multitude of sins, but the Hollywood adage "You're only as good as your last picture" still has a lot of currency. In the case of Zanuck and Brown, their success with *The Sting* had been diluted by a number of subsequent projects: *The Black*

Windmill, The Girl from Petrovka, and *Sugarland Express,* which was directed by Steven Spielberg and starred Goldie Hawn. *Sugarland Express* had been a huge critical success and a disappointment at the box office; it had marked Spielberg's debut in directing features after a brilliant career in television films, where he was already growing tired of being the youngest, hottest new director in Hollywood (he was twenty-six when he made *Sugarland*). Expectations for the film had been high. In time everyone was grateful that *Sugarland* subsequently returned its investment and even turned some profit for the studio, putting it ahead of 90 percent of Hollywood films.

The other three Z and B 1973 projects were less than kindly received by the critics and the public and had shown no signs of taking off at the box office. So, in the summer of 1973, having locked up the film rights to *Jaws,* Zanuck and Brown sat in the south of France, at the Hotel du Cap, and thought about their important new project.

Spielberg, who was in Europe to make personal appearances on behalf of a recently released feature called *Duel,* joined them. Made for American television, *Duel* was a strange, taut adventure story about an encounter between a quiet salesman driving in the Southwest, played by Dennis Weaver, and a menacing monster of a diesel truck that pursues him and deliberately tries to kill him. The TV acclaim for this unusual and well-directed confrontation between a man and a truck led to its release in Europe as a theatrical feature, where it grossed well and enjoyed great critical success, both in the popular press and among the Cahiers du Cinéma crowd as well. Richard, David, and Steven all sat around a cabana on the beach, staring at the Mediterranean and trying to figure out how *Jaws* could become a successful movie.

Steven Spielberg was not originally set as the director of *Jaws,* although his involvement with the picture began when he lifted a copy of the galleys of the book from a desk in the

Zanuck/Brown office and asked if he could read it.[8] He
loved it for its cinematic potential, admired it for its adventure, and said as much. *Sugarland* had been a good experience for all concerned, and there was no reason to
discourage anyone from becoming involved in the new *Jaws*
project. After all, at this point, there was no "package," only
a property. Anyone could play.

Dick and David first considered getting a director who
was a great engineer, one of the old-timers whose principal
virtues are their ability to move the ponderous machinery of
film-making around without hurting the budget or the story
too much. This idea was rejected, and another director considered. The second type was well-known, a good action and
adventure director with proven abilities, but over a long lun-
cheon meeting in New York he kept referring to the malevolent shark of the book as "the whale," and he too was
eventually de-considered.

Meanwhile, Steven was having second thoughts about his
enthusiasm for the book. He was afraid of being typed as an
action director who specialized in contests between brave
men and insensate killers. "Who wants to be known as a
shark-and-truck director?" was his complaint. But the great
shark is hard to ignore, and soon Richard and David formally offered Steven the chance to direct it.

Remember, *Sugarland Express*, Steven's first feature production, hadn't been released yet, and was in its final postproduction stages. Nobody knew how anything was going to
work out. Steven's stated intentions were to take a rest after
the rigors of being on location in Texas for three months
and sweating over the film editing process for three more.
He was under contract to Universal, and he didn't have to
worry where his next picture was coming from. But there
was the temptation to follow the traditional Hollywood
Young Director route and lock up as many commitments as
possible between the completion of his first picture and its
subsequent release.

(There is this grace period when you've earned your spurs by directing a feature, and no one knows what kind of feature it is. With boundless Hollywood optimism, everyone figures you're hot stuff, and you can get more jobs. Later, if your first is a dog, well—it's too late, and besides, you're already on your next, so what the hell. Of course, if you screw up twice in a row, it gets hard to get work, unless you've used the grace period from your second picture to lock up a third. Not a few careers are kept afloat this way. Steven says it's building the bridge in front of you before they burn the ones behind you.)

As a project, *Jaws* was looking better and better: Steven was so entranced with the audience appeal of it, he neglected to worry seriously about possible production problems. Peter was working on the first draft of the script, and Zanuck/Brown kept busy as executive producers of another film based on a major book, Trevanian's *The Eiger Sanction*, a suspense spy thriller which Clint Eastwood was going to do. All in all, it was a busy season.

CHAPTER FOUR

"Let's Make it Real. . . Compared to What?"

(January–February 1974)

All the time they were negotiating for the book, and during autumn of 1973, Dick and David had innocently assumed that they could get a shark trainer somewhere, who, with enough money, could get a great white shark to perform a few simple stunts on cue in long shots with a dummy in the water, after which they could cut to miniatures or something for the close-up stuff. This may sound naive, but remember that Hollywood is a place where they can train dolphins and seagulls, as well as most mammals, to do most anything, and where they can assemble a full combat flight of World War II bombers on a remote airstrip in Guaymas, Mexico. All this without resorting to trick photography or miniatures. Just go see *Day of the Dolphin,* or *Jonathan Livingston Seagull,* or *Catch-22.* It's all possible. It may not turn out the way you'd like it to, especially if you read those books, but that's the movies.

You might not like *Jaws* either. After acquiring the book, and talking to Peter directly, instead of to his agents, Dick and David began to discover otherwise, and Steven commented later that he didn't realize he was getting a novel that would sink its teeth into him. The upshot of it was that in all the world, for all the money and love that Hollywood can offer, there is no one so foolish as to claim to be able to train a shark. They're big, mean, primitive, simple fish; they don't live in captivity, and they are singularly difficult to understand. So much for that aspect of casting. The shark would have to be played a different way.

Steven had been set to direct the picture, pending final contractual commitment. Dick and David would produce; Peter was writing a screenplay that would be a faithful representation of his novel. It was time to take on some help. The Zanuck/Brown company employs a production executive, a man wise in the ways of making pictures whose job it is to be able to anticipate problems, devise solutions, and predict with some certainty the probable costs and schedules of any script put in front of him. This gentleman was Bill Gilmore, and he came on the project almost simultaneously with an art director, Joe Alves,[9] who had just finished *Sugarland*. It was still a family shop, and everyone was used to each other and trusted his fellow's judgment and ability. Joe, a wiry little former race-car driver who reminds me of Foudini in the old TV show *Lucky Pup*, is responsible for the visual design and coordination of whatever is going to appear in front of the camera. If there are sets to be built, he will design them and supervise their construction. If the director and the cinematographer decide everything should look blue, he will see that it looks blue. I'm oversimplifying, but Joe Alves, as much as any art director or production designer in Hollywood, has made a contribution that is unappreciated by folks outside the business, and it's time everyone realized that sets and costumes aren't picked off racks, props don't appear out of a truck, and the visual unity of the physical elements of a film production spring from one special craftsman's mastery of his art.

There is only one artist/craftsman whose art takes precedence, and that's the cinematographer (or cameraman, or director of photography). It's all the same guy, and although his union won't permit him to actually operate the camera, he is ultimately responsible for realizing the director's vision onto the emulsion of the film. He lights the scene, collaborates in the placement of the camera to record that scene, and makes it happen on some kind of realistic schedule, weather permitting. Of course, the director is Boss of All, and if he says "Change it," the cameraman and the art director and everyone else on the set changes it. And that's how most movies get made.

At this point, by December 1, Joe began working on what a shark would look like. He talked to technical experts, he interviewed oceanographers and ichthyologists, he read books, looked at pictures, and began designing the Ultimate Shark, who was, after all, a major star in this picture. It was the title role, right? Shark research is pretty thin stuff, and not much is known about the little darlings. There was one pickled great white which was actually only six feet long and pruning up pretty badly, but you take what you can get. Joe read and reread the book, and talked and talked with Steven, who was beginning to develop his own ideas as to what key sequences might be in the picture. Joe began supervising the rendition of these key sequences into storyboards—elaborate sketches, drawn in a scale frame, illustrating angles and action; essentially, it meant drawing still frames from an imaginary movie that was in the director's head, to the director's demanding specifications.

Throughout the picture, Steven would outline and anticipate pictorial continuity, suggesting camera angles and visual elements, and Joe would see that they were drawn, and drawn again, until Steven was satisfied. It's a large part of any director's preparation, and it would have been nice to do the whole film that way before it got started, but for many complicated reasons, Steven never got the chance to formally "prep" the picture, at least to a degree that would have made him happy. Obviously, he was not so unprepared as all that—in the opinion of others, certainly, he was confident, cool, energetic, and demanding far beyond his years (he was twenty-six when the picture started shooting and about 101 when it ended).

But it soon became evident that The Shark would be a problem. Joe visualized a free-swimming model, with self-contained power, indistinguishable from the real thing on film. Probably full-scale, as well, which meant twenty-six feet long and five or more feet across. A Big Mother Shark. Just to be on the safe side, Steven suggested filming some great white sharks, Bill Gilmore concurred, and lo, it was arranged. Ron and Valerie Taylor, the Australian shark specialists who had photographed the Peter Gimbel documentary *Blue Water, White Death*, were engaged to shoot second-unit footage off the Great Barrier Reef in Australia, where the real sharks hang out.

(Second unit, by the way, is a photographic team that does not shoot principal actors. Second units are responsible for doing all the stuff that the first-unit team is too busy for, like long shots of the yellow car chasing the red car, or beautiful sunsets, or the lion eating the zebra while Farley Granger[10] pretends to be watching, 15,000 miles away on a sound stage draped with plastic vines.)

By this time—it was January 1974—and although the final shooting script was nowhere near completion, it was certain that crucial action sequences would remain in whatever script was finally approved. Specifically, the encounter between Hooper, the young ichthyologist in the book, and the great white shark—the climactic struggle between men and shark that the book is all about—would be in the film. Since chances are we would not be so lucky as to cast an actor to play Hooper who was also a shark expert and an accomplished scuba diver, it looked like a job for second unit. And then we began to see some real creative planning. The villain in the book, the monster shark, is described as being twenty-five feet long. Now, there are few great whites that size. They have been reported that big, but rarely. The chances of the second unit getting onto a boat and finding one were nil. Great whites of ten to fifteen feet were relatively commonplace in Australian waters, but how were we to make them look twice their size? Well, if the sharks aren't going to be big, let's make the actors small . . .

And so Carl Rizzo got a free trip to Australia and almost didn't come back. Carl Rizzo is an ex-jockey, a rugged little guy about 4'9" who used to ride second string to Johnny Longden and raced horses for the likes of Harry James and Betty Grable, for a trainer named William Molter.[11] He got onto a picture as a technical advisor for some horse-racing jockey sequences back in the Fifties, and stayed in, doubling children and young Indians, doing horse falls and other physical stuff too dangerous to risk principals on. He is still an active guy, and hopes someday to own and train and run his own horses out at Del Mar and Santa Anita and Hollywood Park. In the meantime, he's got more than twelve years of stunt work and is working toward a motion picture pension, trying to work the required number of days each year. He was the guy in the diving helmet in the underwater scenes in *Mame*, and when he was asked if he had any diving experience, he naturally answered "Yes." (Actors and others have long ago learned to say "Yes" to any question involved with casting, figuring they can get a few quick lessons in between the time they get the job and the time they actually have to dive, or ride, or fence, or do whatever it is they're going to be asked to do.)

Movie schedules being what they are, Carl Rizzo and a Universal production man left two weeks earlier than expected, and after seventeen hours in a trans-Pacific flight, they shlepped out to Port Lincoln, Australia, and got on a boat to shoot man-eating great white sharks.

It's safe to assume that it's more than Carl Rizzo bargained for, but a job's a job, and he's a pro. On the end of one of the reels of film sent back by the second unit from Australia, there's a cute little home-movie kind of shot, panning from the portico of the Port Lincoln Motel, down to Ron and Valerie Taylor, and a couple of shark cages that were doubles of the one finally used in the film. One of the cages is about 5/8 scale, and another is less than 1/2 scale. The 5/8-size one is for Carl; the little one is loaded with a three-foot doll wearing a perfect little wet suit and teensy air tank, carrying the cutest little spear gun. Carl had his own matching wet suit, with undersize air tanks and miniaturized scuba gear specially made by the Universal Studios special effects shop.

The first week they were lucky, with good weather and plenty of marauding sharks. They lowered the littlest cage, with the doll, and shot a lot of footage of great white sharks biting dead horse hindquarters in half, nosing around the cage, and behaving in a properly threatening manner. Carl is sick from his vaccinations and jet lag, and has had maybe two or three scuba lessons when it's his turn in the cage. The cage is made of tough steel, carefully welded and braced, and it is heavy. Carl gets in, they lower away, and so far everything is fine. Ron and Valerie are in position, in another cage of their own design, with their underwater cameras turning, and here comes a great white, rushing the cage like it's a free lunch. Carl chokes up a little, loses his regulator (the device that controls the flow of air from his tanks), forgets how to clear the water from a filled breathing mouthpiece, and is trapped in this cage surrounded by about 1,200 pounds of hungry shark snapping away. Panic sets in, he pulls his safety line, frantically signaling "Take me up," and they begin to winch him in. Unfortunately for Carl, the cage is so heavy that the little auxiliary powerboat responsible for him is having a hard time getting the cage out of the water, which is too bad for Carl, since as long as he's in the cage, he's safe from the shark, but he's not safe from being underwater without air. Eventually, they distract the shark, get the cage up, and Carl is a little shaken up but not incapacitated. Fortunately, they've run out of blood and dead horse, so it's time to head back for Port Lincoln to stock up on bait.

Now they're out again, but the weather's a little rougher than before and it's getting hard to find the sharks. Carl makes a few dives, getting used to the scuba gear and learning how to clear his mask and regulator. But there's no usable film, so it's heigh-ho, back to port, then out again. This time, they're filming off an underwater area known worldwide as Dangerous Reef. Appropriate, no? Carl is feeling pretty good, Ron and Valerie Taylor and their crew are happy, but there's some trouble with local abalone divers, who are grumpy about shark bait getting loose and into the fishing grounds. (Keep in mind the national sport in Australia is punching people, so some surly abalone divers off Port Lincoln and Dangerous Reef are probably a little hairier than they are off Carmel, California.)

But movies must be made, and eventually a big mean great white appears, really hungry for some week-old dead livestock and fish heads. Well, as soon as he's sighted, out comes Carl's 5/8-scale cage, and his cute little air tanks and scuba gear and ineffectual little spear gun, and it's over the side for the chap. Only the shark is not waiting for anyone to say "Action." He's got two or three million years of evolution saying "Lunchtime!" and pointing at the commotion on the surface, where Carl is trying to enter the cage from the top so they can fasten it down and send him under. Then the shark goes for Carl and the cage and gives the whole arrangement a mighty gnashing of teeth and a great lashing of tail, and Carl is bashed out of the cage onto the boat. The shark gets tangled in the lines, half in and half out of the water, and begins to tear things up. A 1,500-pound great white can bite through oak planking, flatten things with his tail, and generally create more fuss than an army of beer-crazed Australian abalone divers. He can also kill you quicker than you can bite a cocktail frank, and in much the same way. In the second-unit footage shot with the surface camera, you can see the folks in the auxiliary launch scrambling to avoid the mighty tail, with taut nylon lines popping like thread and scraps of aluminum and steel and wood flying through the air. The steel cage sinks to the bottom, with no one sure if Carl is in it or not. If he's under in it, he's got to stay there for fear of being gobbled. If he's under *out of it*, he's a goner. If he's under *in it*, he's also in deep trouble because his little 5/8-scale air tanks only hold a little 5/8-scale air supply, assuming he's remembered to clear his mask and keep his regulator straight. Fortunately, the shark breaks free without killing anyone, although the solid steel cage is totaled by the action and brought up from the bottom in pieces.

Carl is intact, but here's where stories differ. According to Carl, he was shaken up pretty bad, but he realized it was like getting thrown off a horse or going through the rail—you've got to get back on. So he went down a few times after that. According to anonymous reports, the next time Carl was scheduled to dive, he was nowhere to be found, which is no mean trick on a thirty-five-foot fishing boat. It makes a better story to say he was located cowering in the forward chain lockers with the anchor, developing a drinking problem and going home vowing to never dive again, or even eat seafood. But when I talked to him in a neat little Hollywood apartment, he related simply that they went back to port because of bad weather and to repair their damaged equipment, and went out again without incident a week later. But adverse weather and complaints by abalone divers scrubbed further shooting, and everyone flew home with the footage they had. Carl had high praise for Rodney Fox, who crewed with Ron and Valerie Taylor. Fox has the distinction of being one of the only men ever to survive a full shark attack—and he has the incredible scars to prove it. (Rodney is the guy in *Blue Water, White Death* with the neat outline of shark tooth marks defining a bite radius that encompasses his entire upper-left torso and shoulder. He owns the Port Lincoln Motel, where everyone stayed, and he still fools around with sharks.)

The second-unit Australian shark footage was now complete, and it would be a year and a half before we knew if it would work in the film, if the angles and color and ocean and props would match the shooting that was to come. It was a $100,000 gamble on Bill Gilmore's part, and it paid off. Steven had sketched sixteen specific angles and shots he wanted; Ron and Valerie worked from those as closely as they could, and when you see the picture you'll never be able to guess what footage was shot where. Carl Rizzo, of course, will never forget it.

This may all sound terribly elaborate, but it's important to remember that Steven's directorial sense demanded that this film be shot with all the principals in the frame. That meant that the usual movie magic couldn't be used—no long shots of a shark intercut with close-ups of faces reacting, no cutaways to miniatures, no models. The story and the movie required that you see a boat, and men, and a shark, all in the same shot, on the surface of an ocean with an open horizon. Further, underwater, you'd have to see a man in a shark cage being attacked by a giant shark. Movies have come a long way in terms of realism, and new fast film stocks and advances in lighting have made location filming a part of the moviegoer's visual vocabulary, and the days of shooting everything on a back lot or soundstage are just about over. Compared to shooting at sea, a mock-up of a boat in front of a projection of the ocean rocked by off–camera hands looks phony, no matter how much water is thrown on the actors by a prop man. Our Australian footage shows real sharks snapping at a live human. The illusion so necessary to the story is honestly arrived at, even though it remains illusion. Richard Dreyfuss was never in the water with a live shark, but folks scream just the same, because somewhere, someone was nose-to-nose with a great white, and a camera was turning nearby.

Meanwhile, back in Los Angeles, Joe Alves has designed the exterior of the Ultimate Shark and lovingly built a model that can fit on top of a desk. It's clean, accurate, and dangerous-looking. Dr. Leonard Compagno, a technical advisor and expert in the species, comes down and pronounces it as good as anything he's ever seen, alive or dead, real or imagined. When the giant is constructed, he will marvel again and wistfully remark that no school or museum could afford to build so grand a model to such magnificent proportions with such precision and detail. It just goes to show what the Smithsonian might do, if it only had the money. But being big and being perfect-looking is not enough. The giant must move in the water convincingly and do what it's called upon to do by the script—which is not yet completed to everyone's satisfaction—and by the director, who will make demands based on art, not on science. There must be a way to breathe life into the fish, without going back to Genesis and calling upon the Almighty to "create great whales and every living creature that moveth, which the waters brought forth abundantly." Even Universal Studios would hesitate at that, although in all fairness, it should be noted that the special effects department was consulted.

The artists and engineers and craftsmen in Hollywood are the best in the world at what they do, and over the years their miracles have thrilled and delighted millions upon millions of moviegoers all over the world. They are an older breed now, and some of them are retiring without passing on their skills, for without the studio system of production there isn't enough steady work to justify the long apprenticeship that's required to make a first-class special effects man. A lot of guys around can blow up cars and detonate explosive squibs to simulate bullet hits, but the real masters are steadily dwindling in number; someday, like the dodo and the contract starlet, they too will become extinct, although one hopes that this won't be so.[12]

Universal, being a big studio with a lot of ongoing activity, supports one of the best special effects shops in the industry, and the 1974 Oscars (for *Earthquake*) are testimony to their skills. But in late 1973 and early 1974, they took a look at the shark that Joe Alves had designed and shook their heads.

Models were suggested. Miniatures to be built by Japanese masters at Toho Studios in the Orient. Maybe full animation, matted into the picture. But a real life-size shark? Forget it.

In their defense, it should be pointed out that the special effects guys at Universal put a low priority on the project. For a while, everyone did. The book was just being published, nobody knew the property except those closest to it, the explosive best-seller *Jaws* was still months away from any reality, and there were a couple of big projects very much in the works: *Airport '75*, *Earthquake*, and *Hindenburg* were all in advanced stages of preparation. To a shop busy trying to burn a zeppelin, crash a Boeing 747 in midair, and destroy the entire city of Los Angeles, a twenty-five-foot shark was no urgent case. Besides, it probably couldn't be done. And here, we come to the crux of the problem. In many ways, launching *Jaws* was a film production problem analogous to NASA trying to land men on the moon and bring them back. It just had never been done.

Let me repeat that. The production requirements of the shark action sequences in *Jaws* had never been done before.

Not in seventy-five years of movie-making. Not in the time of D. W. Griffith or Cecil B. DeMille. *Earthquake?* Cities have been made to tumble before. Almost everything has been done somewhere once before—just think of all the movies you've ever seen or heard about: giant gorillas climbing the Empire State Building, hordes of cavalry, heathen temples, parting the Red Sea, invaders from Mars destroying Los Angeles; somewhere, almost everything's been done. But nobody had ever built a working realistic photo double of a twenty-five-foot great white shark that could swim, be photographed from all angles, and perform certain tricks, like biting a man in two, attacking a boat, suffering strikes from harpoons and missiles, and generally being the meanest monster since The Mummy walked and Jack Palance put on black gloves in *Shane*. Through the industry grapevine, and by way of a model-maker who knew his work, we found that the only man who seemed suited for the job was retired. A veteran of forty years in pictures, he apprenticed to his father in the good old days and spent his first years working at the old Douglas Fairbanks Studios, after helping his father build the gold coins and finely wrought props used in the first *King of Kings*. His name was Bob Mattey, and he's the guy who made those little rocket ships fly around sputtering sparks in the old *Flash Gordon* serials.

More to the point, Bob Mattey had worked at the Disney Studios for seventeen years before his retirement, and Disney, like Universal, is one of the last remaining working studios with continuity of personnel. There, Bob Mattey had supervised the Fred MacMurray flying machine and designed and operated the fabulous undersea effects that thrilled us in *20,000 Leagues Under the Sea*. Remember the hand-to-hand combat between the men of the *Nautilus* and the giant squid? Bob Mattey built and operated that squid, and it was the closest anyone had been to our giant shark. He was presented with the problem, and he took it home with him with a "let's see what we can do here" attitude, which was 100 percent more optimistic than any other approach to the problem to date. Besides, who else in Hollywood had a garage full of working fake alligators, including a radio-controlled fifteen-footer? They had been built for the old Tarzan pictures, and you never can tell when you'll need a working alligator, so there they were, gathering dust, just waiting to slither down the bank and into the water, should Johnny Weismueller ever return.

But the alligators were only an indication of what the old master could do when called upon. He came out of retirement, put aside his plans to build a cabin in the mountains, and went to work on making the giant shark work. His enthusiasm was a welcome change from the others consulted on the job. In a week or so Bob Mattey was back at the studio with a group of little models, which he demonstrated. Carefully welded out of steel and copper rods and lovingly put together, they were: a submersible platform with a track, on which rode a cranelike attachment with a bucket-pivot on top; a model of a fishing boat with flotation barrels supporting a realistic superstructure; and a little shark that fitted onto the pivot arm that rode on the track on the submersible platform. What we were looking at was eventually to weigh twelve tons, require a crew of fifteen men to operate, and cause a lot of people a lot of grief. It looked so cute on a tabletop, and so practical. In the end, it would make the shark work like gangbusters and the crew curse like demons. Sometimes it wouldn't work at all, and that was called "technical problems," and in the months to come, the technical problems would cost Universal Studios more than a couple of million dollars—enough to make *American Graffiti* three times, and enough to make a lot of executives think long and hard about the project.

But in the winter of 1973–74, *Jaws* was swimming right along—the shark looked OK, and while Zanuck and Brown toured the country to promote the opening of one of their other films, the welders and artisans began construction of Universal's own great white shark. On a big project like *Jaws,* or any film that's going to be a big-budget item, the studio go-aheads come in pieces. David Brown comments that most projects get a firm green light about two weeks after principal photography has begun, and in a way, he's right. Any time before the crews and actors go to work and the camera starts to turn, a picture can be scrubbed, at enormous expense, but always for less than it would cost to go ahead and shoot. *Jaws* was no exception. One of the early signs of studio involvement was the authorization to go ahead and build the shark. The second was an OK to scout locations— and I'll get into this in a minute. First, a word about the script.

Peter Benchley had been through about three drafts now, often with Steven making suggestions that he felt would help make it a cinematic experience, as opposed to a literary

one. Peter is interested and keen to learn; he's interested in
doing more films, and has since succeeded in placing several other original screenplays, bypassing the novel part in
favor of plunging directly into motion pictures. But the *Jaws*
script was not yet right, and Steven and Dick and David sat
fretting over it. There are some elements of the novel that
seem to cry out for change, a subplot to be eliminated, and
an overall filmic thrust yet to be developed. Enter Prestigious Writer Number Two, who has asked for and been
granted anonymity.[13] The author of a Broadway smash of a
few seasons back later transformed into a successful film, he
is a diver by avocation, lives on an island when he's not writing, and knows oceans and the abundant life therein. He is
in Hollywood between assignments, awaiting the verdict on
a screenplay he's done for Peter Bogdanovich, which at this
writing is not yet a movie. In the four weeks he's got, he offers to do a rewrite on *Jaws*. So it's off into a room at the
good ol' Bel Air Hotel, for an intensive rewrite—again with
Steven supervising and suggesting. And while this is going
on, Joe Alves is out looking for a place to shoot.

Jaws has some unique location requirements: an obvious
summer resort town that derives 90 percent of its income in
the twelve-week summer season, full of picturesque and pho-
togenic features. So far, easy. Now, recall the twelve-ton steel
submersible platform for the shark. This must operate in
twenty-five to thirty-five feet of water with a level, sandy bottom. Now you've got some limits to work within. But wait. In
addition, there must be a sheltered bay in the lee of an island, so that the camera can point out to 180 degrees of unbroken horizon and still be protected from vagaries of wind
and weather and mid-ocean swells. Further, the tide must be
within manageable limits, preferably no more than two to
three feet during normal seasons. Which rules out every Hollywood production man's first choice, Santa Catalina, which
has five- to six-foot tides. And, finally, all this natural beauty—
sheltered anchorage, level sandy bottom, and optimum

depth and tides—all this must be within a forty-five-minute drive or sail from a hotel complex capable of housing and feeding a feature film crew of more than 100 men and women, not counting stars and above-the-line personnel like producers and directors, who require special handling.

Joe Alves began with maps of the world, and narrowed that down to the continental United States, for starters. If that wouldn't work out, he was prepared to start looking into the Azores and off the coast of Africa, but let's not make things more complicated than they are, right? He meets Peter Benchley in New York and hears his ideas since, after all, it's Peter's book and first-draft screenplay. Long Island is what's indicated, so Joe begins scouting Long Island, cruising every town from the Hamptons out to Montauk Point. It's not right. So he starts in with his coast and geodetic survey charts and marine surveys and begins to look at the New England coast, working down Cape Cod and Rhode Island, hitting every closed-for-the-winter clam bar and Captain's Shanty there. Martha's Vineyard is on the map, but Joe is advised to bypass it and instead is invited to dinner with Peter's parents on Nantucket Island, where Nathaniel Benchley wrote a hit novel called *The Off-Islanders,* which was made into the successful movie *The Russians Are Coming* (filmed in northern California). On the way to Nantucket, the ferry is turned back because of foul weather, and Joe decides to check out Martha's Vineyard as long as he's there. Well, it's perfect. Cute town, quaint streets, nice beaches, and moderate tides. Let's check the charts . . . Oh boy! Twenty-six-foot sandy bottom. And there's Cow Bay, looking out to sea, sheltered in the lee of the island, and fifteen minutes from the hotels in Edgartown. It's all buried under a couple of feet of snow, which is unusual for the island, but what the hell; it's a beautiful location. Joe takes a mess of pictures, and flies back to Los Angeles to tell the guys.

Bill Gilmore, Steven, and Joe fly back, and they drive and walk all over the island, picking potential locations. Steven flies back to L.A. to work on the script, then returns to check out a boat that Joe has found in a Boston shipyard, a forty-two-foot Nova Scotia lobster boat named *Warlock* that will be remade and refitted to play the part of the professional shark fisherman's vessel, and be the stage for a significant part of the film's action. Bob Mattey comes along, since his special effects crew will have to rig this boat for a number of effects, and during the tour, he slips and cracks his head on the icy boatyard ground. "Are you OK, Bob?" "I'm fine, Joe." "Where are your glasses, Bob?" "I don't wear glasses, Joe . . ." But Bob Mattey *always* wears glasses, so it's off to the hospital to see if he's got a concussion. He hasn't, but it's a portent. But then, who knew? It was a sign, all right, and not just for Bob Mattey.

CHAPTER FIVE

"Ready, Get Set, Get Set, Get Set . . ."

(March 1974)

Steven commented, after it was all over, that waiting for a firm date for *Jaws* was like being in a race, keyed up and on the blocks, straining, waiting for the gun, and listening to the starter give you one of these: "Ready, get set, get set . . . Are you ready? OK. Get set . . . Are you on your mark? Good . . . Ready? Get set . . . you can start now." And then, four months later, a plaintive "Are you done yet?"

The release of a major motion picture is a carefully planned event, timed to coincide with historically proven periods of peak attendance, like Christmas and the summer, and to satisfy the distributor's requirements for a full schedule, and to meet the exhibitor's needs for product to play in his theaters, which is why few "blockbusters" open in the wet months of late winter and why a studio will try not to fight itself by releasing pictures of similar theme or exploitable elements against each other. Since you've got to battle for playing-time anyway, better to battle the other studios. Sometimes, this competition can work against everyone: three well-made movies about outlaw couples on the run from organized society were released nearly simultaneously last year, by three different distributors/studios, and they all died—Steven's *Sugarland Express,* Terry Malik's *Badlands,* and Robert Altman's *Thieves Like Us.* Any one of them might have had an individual success, but I think they split the ticket and divided the market, and everyone suffered.[14]

In the case of *Jaws* it was obvious there would be no competing pictures with similar thematic content—the novel was too extraordinary for that, and the problems, as we were finding out, were insurmountable to a low-budget operation, which is where a quickie rip-off might come from.

In the case of *Jaws* the Zanuck/Brown Company and Universal believed the picture should probably be a summer release (a favored time), which was consistent with the picture's theme and content. So finishing was no problem. June of 1975 was a long way from February of 1974, or so everyone thought. The company was looking for an April start, hoping to finish shooting in the Martha's Vineyard location before the summer season swamped the island, increasing problems for a company on location. There were housing costs to think of—the Vineyard is a prime Eastern resort area, and the rooms that went begging for $14 a night in the off-season would be $45 and hard to get when the tourists started arriving. There'd be problems of crowd control, availability of local labor, escalating per diem costs for feeding the company—it could all add up to a big headache.

There were further doubts about the "legs" of the book. *Jaws,* the novel, despite all the work and planning that had gone into its writing and in its presale to paperback and book clubs, was just released: the reviews were money reviews, and it looked good for the book, but nobody knew how good. First, it would have to become a best-seller. Then, it would have to stay on the best-seller lists and sell enough copies to generate some healthy interest. And then, when the hardcover and book-club market had been saturated, the paperback edition would come out. In the best of all possible worlds, the peak of the paperback sales period would coincide with the release date of the picture somehow, so that all those folks who just bought the book would be interested in seeing the movie. But the book had broken nationally only in late January, and without knowing how long it would last, everyone was anxious to get the movie wrapped as soon as possible so that an early release might be effected if the book failed to have staying power.

Well, not to worry. *The New York Times* book reviewer concluded a mixed notice with the admonition "Read *Jaws*—by all means read it . . ." The others were pretty much the same: the booksellers had ordered well; in-store displays were set; and the book, not unpredictably, started to climb up the best-seller list, coming in at tenth place on March 10 and climbing to number three the following week. The hardcover edition stayed on the best-seller list for an impressive forty-four weeks, which means more than just being a literary success. The paperback edition finally made it all the way to number one. But we'll be back to the significance of that long run as a best-seller in a while. In the context of February and March 1974, the pressure was to get the movie made.

By now, Writer Number Two had finished his contributions, and the written and rewritten script was in its fourth draft. Many of Steven's changes had been incorporated into it, and the studio was happy. Richard Zanuck and David Brown were less happy, and Steven was least happy of all. But the studio's pleasure meant that they could begin the serious work of budgeting and boarding the picture. This was a joint undertaking of the executive production people, with the studio represented by a wise veteran of many production wars named Marsh Green.

Bill Gilmore, months earlier, had read a twelve-page synopsis of the novel and said "Sure" when he was asked could it be done. Now it was time for everyone concerned to sit down and figure out, as closely as humanly possible, for how much and how long. Richard Zanuck would pore over estimates and proposals, and Steven would get right in there and rumble along with them, trying to assure himself adequate time and money to do the job right, fighting for every extra day's shooting. If anything had come out of the exhaustive analysis and rewritings of the basic story, it was that the film had a three-act structure, like a well-made play. The first two acts were played on land, and with the exception of a couple of shark attacks in which the monster would only be hinted at and never fully revealed, there was nothing to cause any production man any concern. It was straightforward movie-making, telling a story, using actors and scenery, working outdoors and indoors, all on location. That part was easy. With the accumulated wisdom and experience of hundreds of films behind them, all parties concerned could look at the proposed budget and agree: "Yes, that's about right—one day here, two days here, a week on the beach, three days with 400 extras," and like that. But the crucial third act, in which the three men go to sea in the fishing boat and confront the great white—well, that hadn't been done before, not "live" on location with a fourteen-ton shark mechanism and a full crew.

There are two elements to the physical planning of a feature film. One is the budget; the second is the production board. The production board is a unique planning device, difficult to visualize if you've never seen one. For now, let me describe it as a collection of movable cardboard strips, each one representing a day's shooting and summarizing the actors required, the pages of the script to be shot, and the physical location. When laid out in sequence, these little strips of cardboard show the projected progress of the picture, from the first day of shooting to the last, and the physical moves and requirements of every day. Because of the nature of the film business, the little cardboard strips are movable, interchangeable, color-coded, and never frozen into position, since any day anything can change and every change affects everything that is to come. On *Jaws*, the poor board never got a rest, and the biggest folding board made couldn't accommodate the little cardboard strips, each one representing one day and $50,000, on a rough average. That's the cost of a distant location's shooting, whether or not any usable film results.

A movie budget is like any other—so much for salary, so much for overhead, for rental of equipment, for room and board for the crew, for the costs of building things or renting them, etc. Richard Zanuck makes a very good analogy between film budgets and par on a golf course. It's supposed to be a kind of golden mean, the average strokes needed for a competent player to reach the flag. You supply your own handicap. Dick Zanuck commented later that trying to figure par for *Jaws* was like playing with new clubs on a strange course with an exploding ball. In movies, the budget is divided by a line. Those "above the line" are the producers and director, the writer(s), the actors, the purchase of the story material—the "talent," so to speak. "Below the line" is where the technicians dwell, along with the physical production costs, the insurance, and the many miscellaneouses that arise to plague the profit-and-loss statement and final audit.

Par for *Jaws* was estimated at around $3.5 million, although the exact amount is one of the most closely guarded secrets in the film industry. I'm not copping out here, it's just that hardly anybody really knows what a picture costs except a very few top-level studio heads and the actual producers, and that's true of every picture, no matter where it's made. There are very complex reasons for this, most of them having to do with the eventual profits a film may make and the subsequent division of those profits. There have been many bitter recriminations over budgets after the fact, when the film rental dollars have all been banked and it's time for someone to know, "Did we break even? Did we lose? Did we win? How much?" How much, in Hollywood, is none of anyone's business.[15]

This is tradition, practice, and custom, and it's not going to change here. Anyway, $3.5 million is close enough for starters. That figure would pay for around fifty-five days of filming, plus the additional second-unit work to round out the action sequences. Roughly thirty-five of those days were to be on land, with the remaining twenty to be spent at sea. But, as Dick Zanuck remarked some months afterward, "People applied every known assumption to something that had never been done before."

Over at Rolly Harper's, a large-scale catering operation that specializes in feeding movie companies on location, there was some unused work space; and there it was that welders and mechanics were putting together the immense mechanism that was to be the underpinning and core of the shark's role in the picture. To date, about $100,000 had been spent in Australia; the shark was budgeted for another $175,000 or so, not counting operators, transportation, and location costs; and the book had cost a basic $150,000, plus another $50,000 or $75,000 for script development. Say a half million, so far, and no start date set. (This may sound extravagant, but it's not. Many pictures have been much deeper into expenses before any shooting started.) But $500,000 does indicate one thing—somebody, somewhere, was serious about making this picture, and time was slipping by.

During this period of slippage (it was March 23), Steven was frankly getting worried. A director's preparation should be extensive and thorough; a film just doesn't spring full-blown onto celluloid. Preparations should include (but not be limited to) having illustrations made for pictorial continuity, anticipating camera angles and visual elements, analyzing the script scene by scene to determine director's choices such as point of view, theme, story points, and relationship of characters and their movement in the frame. All esoteric stuff, but very necessary.

The three-sided relationship between Richard, David, and Steven became more intense as the weeks went by, with everybody taking turns not talking to each other. Steven would threaten to leave the project. Richard would argue. David would reason. Steven would return, but on conditions. Most of the conditions would be met, some would later be forgotten.

The turbulent bubbling of preproduction anxiety would be periodically interrupted as Steven would be called away to check progress on the shark, to fly East to look at locations in Martha's Vineyard, to attend to the details of his private life, to confer with the production department about technical problems. The picture wasn't even at sea and already there were waves washing up around people's ankles. None of this is unusual, but it is nerve-wracking and it contributes to the irritability which often is evident during the process of film-making. To everyone's credit, an outward calm was preserved, and the overall tone of preproduction was supportive and mutually helpful. After all, everyone was trying to work hard to make the movie happen before the book faded away, and the principals had already been through some of these trials together on another picture.

The book refused to fade. Quite the contrary. Week after week, it kept on selling, and pretty soon it became evident that Universal and Zanuck/Brown had a substantial hit on their hands. It is estimated that the hardcore hardcover book buyers in this country number around 60,000; these are the folks who want to read books when they are new; they make the best-sellers. When they're through buying, it's usually time to hit the masses at the airports and the drugstores with the paperback version. But *Jaws* showed signs of exceeding this basic upper limit, which indicated that most delightful of prospects—people were buying the novel who normally didn't buy books. That meant a genuine grass-roots movement toward the property. This was a film that had to be made, whatever the problems to be surmounted and the cost in blood, sweat, tears, and dollars.

The project had an all-powerful ally in MCA/Universal President Sid Sheinberg, whose interest and affection for it extended even down to inspection trips to Rolly Harper's to check the progress of the shark mechanism. As production problems mounted, the soothing waves of publisher's reports calmed the furrowed executive brows in the Universal Tower.

I first met Steven Spielberg some years ago, when our mutual agent had married us on a happy collaboration that went nowhere, but looked very good for a short time. We had written this great outline for a film, had this great meeting at Warner Brothers, where we generated a great response. The agent stipulated quite firmly that if they liked the idea so much, they could just count on having Steven direct it if it became a "go"' project. Since Steven was twenty-two years old, the youngest member of the Directors' Guild, and at home behind the camera, that condition was the rock on which the project foundered, despite his clearly evident talents. But we stayed friends, even after the agent left us both, and we discussed art and the industry from time to time. Occasionally I would play a small part as an actor in something Steven would be directing as a television movie, generally improvising my own dialogue, and chiming in with suggestions about the stories he'd be slaving to finish on-time and on-budget. It was easy for me: I was only there for a few days, saying some simple words. He had to make the damn things. But it was good practice for what was to come, and I believe we enjoyed each other's company and professional opinions.

In March Steven sent me the *Jaws* script and asked me what part I thought I could play. I leaped in with Harry Meadows, the publisher of the Amity newspaper, who somewhat resembles me in his appetites. It wasn't a big part, but it was there, and I thought I could do it justice. Besides, we'd be working together on location, and Steven's inclination is to let actors have their way with dialogue in rehearsals, allowing characters to improvise entire scenes. This process leads director and writer to a more natural sound, generating a liveliness and realism that is sometimes missing in these parts. I could help with that, we decided, since I'd be on location.

It seemed to me like a good thing to do. I was working at this time as creative consultant on a weekly situation comedy, rewriting other writers, hammering out script problems, trying to get characters to work, all within the very exacting limitations imposed by the weekly format: a filmed-live three-camera show based on a Neil Simon Broadway hit.[16] These shows are filmed in their entirety in correct sequence in front of a live audience, and live laughs have to be bought and paid for, not borrowed from a laugh track or "sweetening" machine.

I had begun my show-business career in an improvisational revue called The Committee, in San Francisco, stage-managing, directing, and finally acting. I had come to Hollywood with the show, been hired out of it to write for the old CBS *Glen Campbell Summer Show*, and had gone on to write for the Smothers Brothers during their last good TV season in 1968–69, winning an Emmy in the process. When CBS dropped the show I stayed in Los Angeles, writing for television, selling screenplays, acting, producing and directing commercials, and generally keeping afloat with what I hoped was good work.

When I had read the script a few more times, I sent Steven a long note, outlining my reactions. I thought it would make a great popular entertainment, I expressed fears that it would turn into another *Poseidon Adventure* or *Airport*, with cardboard characters doing plastic things, and I expressed hope that if it realized its full potential, the oceans of the world would be as devoid of swimmers as showers were after Alfred Hitchcock had Janet Leigh stabbed to death in the Bates Motel in *Psycho*. In short, I said, "It's almost there, and if you can cast the shark right, and get a good tame stunt-double shark to do the close-in stuff with the actors, you've got a monster on your hands (box-office-wise, as they say)." That's what we hoped. I also enclosed three pages of specific objections, praises, and comments. After all, what are friends for? I figured I already had the part of Meadows, so at least I could speak freely and then be around to watch what would happen to the film, since I'd be there.

In the next few weeks, we'd be talking about the picture whenever Steven could spare time from his preparation, sharing a lunch or some sushi at a local Japanese restaurant. There we were, eating fish, and soon enough the sea would have its revenge, and fish would be gnawing at both our guts. But in late March and early April we had a few laughs. Ha, ha.

In the Universal Tower and in the production department, pressure was mounting. The studio wanted a firm start-date, and had started talking about April 10. "Impossible," said Steven. Zanuck/Brown suggested April 20. Nope. How about July 1? Absolutely not, too late. Everyone was wondering if the book would slip, and there was an internal momentum to keep up. Once a picture is set rolling, it gathers speed and volume, like a snowball. Sets are being constructed, costumes and props ordered, a cast assembled, and the million details are being codified and organized into manageable physical elements. Trucks are ready to roll, key personnel are hired and told to stand by, and a lot of attention is paid in geometrically increasing amounts as the start date draws near.

Movie-making is a rare phenomenon in our mechanized age, a gut-level, instinctual activity where individual reactions and responses are acted on; Dick Zanuck felt strongly that he could not break the roll, not halt the flow, not block the momentum of the project. It had to happen, and it had to happen soon. May 2 was finally set as the start. This would allow a fifty-five-day schedule for principal photography (first-unit, full-crew stuff with stars and actors), and another couple of weeks for second-unit stuff, with a week for underwater stunt things with the shark (all this in addition to the Australian footage already in the can). It was less than Steven wanted, but the budget had been taking $500,000 jumps up and down, yo-yoing between $3 million and $4.5 million dollars. The $3.5 million budget and its production schedule were finally approved, and if everything went right, principal photography on Martha's Vineyard would be completed around the end of June, before high season rates took a chokehold on the per diems, and in time to avoid a potential actors' strike.

A what? An actors' strike. The Screen Actors Guild had a contract which was going to expire on July 1, 1974,[17] and there were some clear indications that certain elements of the old contract would be unacceptable to the new, militant leadership of the union. Although it's hard to think of above-the-line stars who earn more than $100,000 a picture as "labor," they are SAG members, and it is their cooperation that gives the union its ultimate clout. SAG has won many important battles over the years, and the "million a picture plus 10 percent of the gross" star follows the same working rules as the scale day-player with a silent bit. To any major production, a potential SAG strike is something to consider.

Anyway, there was this actors' strike that might happen July 1, and everybody was worried about it. No studio wanted to have a major feature in production if that were to occur since the havoc caused by the interruption of shooting would be not only monumental, but catastrophic. Stars might not be carrying picket signs and shouting "Huelga," but they would not be showing up for work, and there's not that much to keep a hundred-man crew busy with when the actors aren't around. *Jaws* was no exception.

CHAPTER SIX

"Who Can We Get to Play the Part of . . ."

(April 1974)

Soon enough it was April, and the picture was taking shape. It had to.

I was playing the character of Meadows the publisher, a part which was later cut considerably, leaving Murray Hamilton, as Mayor Vaughn, to carry the burden of being the Heavy. In the final cut of the picture, I'm there, helping the cover-up, but not in what you'd call an Academy Award— winning performance. As the writer, it was my sad duty to write myself out of the picture as superfluous, and as an actor, my heart bled with every cut. Talk about ego splits— you haven't experienced schizophrenia until you sit in a story conference discussing whether your presence in a scene is necessary or desirable, knowing that every cut you make as a writer destroys you as an actor and that every objection you raise has to be judged on two levels: the writer's defense of a character in a scene, and the actor's dismay at being eliminated from a juicy role. I finally overcame my discomfort and wrote for the story, not for myself.

Murray Hamilton had been cast as Larry Vaughn, the smoothly corrupt but genuinely sincere mayor of the fictional resort town of Amity. A unanimous choice, he was the first actor set. Competent and gifted with an uncanny ability to portray weakness posing as strength, Murray was a natural for the part.[18] He had played similar villains before, but in *Jaws* he would be the foremost spokesman for the "rational" view, as well as the defender of the town's economy and architect of the cover-up. Quite coincidentally, he bears a passing resemblance to Richard Nixon, and would be a natural choice to play the part of the Boy From Whittier, should that film ever be made. In the novel, Mayor Vaughn carried a subplot that linked him to the Mafia, but that complication had long been cut from the script, and he was now a far more direct victim of his own inability to see the truth.

Another steamy subplot that had been excised in creating the movie was the love affair between the police chief's wife and the young oceanographer. The sexual tension created by that liaison had been eliminated in favor of a more straightforward approach to the storytelling, an uncomplicated man-against-shark monster/adventure yarn with overtones of social conscience and individual action for the common good throughout. An actress named Lorraine Gary[19] was selected to play the wife, a character who has to be a perfect complement to the actor who would play Martin Brody, the complex and determined chief of police for the resort community. Lorraine was sweet, vulnerable, and carried a hint of toughness that would cement the audience's understanding of the relationship between herself and Brody. Ironically, we later dropped the social backgrounds of the novel and invented new back-stories that would serve better to explain Martin and Ellen's behavior and attitudes.

The casting of Martin Brody was an important choice. Though only one of the trio of stars in the picture, he would be the one who is on-screen almost throughout the entire story, and his character was the most complex. He would have to begin as a man who lets others shape his decisions, even to the point where those decisions cost people their lives; he would have to discover his flaw, struggle to correct it, and emerge at the end of the picture as a man who has faced up to the demons inside him and conquered them, while at the same time subjecting himself to the gruesomest sort of physical danger. Naturally, it was a much sought-after part. Quite early on, Zanuck and Brown had made an important casting decision. Curiously enough, it went counter to their choices on other pictures, and, to their credit, it must be said that their choice was determined by what would be best for the picture. In *The Sting* they had elected superstar casting, matching Paul Newman and Robert Redford for the first lime since *Butch Cassidy*. Now, with another potentially big best-seller property, they determined to go in a different direction. Steven agreed that the symbolic "importance" of name stars with familiar box-office faces would detract from the story, and he and Zanuck/Brown decided to go with actors whose ability and correctness would serve the plot without causing the audience to subconsciously murmur to itself, "Look, isn't that Steve McQueen cute? I love the way he wrinkles his nose," or whatever it is that audiences say when they see Steve McQueen. (By the way, it's an old producer's cop-out to say "The story is the star," when what they mean is, "We've spent too much on the script, so we're going to cut a few corners with unknowns." But in the case of *Jaws*, the final casting choices were no bargain-basement remnants, and their unique abilities and warm interaction made the script come alive with added meanings. You can't write the kind of interaction that the cast brought to the picture, and speaking as the author of many of the words they spoke I was thoroughly pleased by the result.) Charlton Heston wanted very much to play Brody, but he had just saved a 747 jetliner in *Airport '75* and he was going to save Los Angeles in *Earthquake*, and it just didn't seem right for him to be wasting his time with a little New England resort community.

So Roy Scheider, an early favorite of Steven's, got the part, and first billing.[20] He was known primarily for his icy competence in the portrayal of tough New York cops, first as

Gene Hackman's partner in *The French Connection* and later as the tough undercover cop in *The Seven-Ups*. The part of Brody was a welcome change from plainclothes Superman, and we worked long and hard to develop a rounded, deeper character.

There were two leads left to cast when the picture was three weeks away from that May 2 start date. We couldn't wait for someone's availability, so the range of possible players was narrowing down. Many of the actors the producers, director, and studio thought about had commitments that would interfere with start-and-stop times. We were looking for a Matt Hooper, the young ichthyologist and oceanographer who represents civilization and education and modern science; and a Quint, the eccentric, complex professional fisherman with an ingrained hatred for all sharks, a professional sharker who kills the beasts for pleasure as well as gain, and provides the brute, animal cunning that first snags the monster in the story.

For Hooper, there were actors like Timothy Bottoms, the intelligent and sincere law student in *Paper Chase*; Jeff Bridges, a handsome young actor of proven ability and charm; and Richard Dreyfuss, the intellectual in *American Graffiti*. He was later highly visible in a poorly made but intense starring vehicle called *The Apprenticeship of Duddy Kravitz*, a kind of Canadian *Catcher in the Rye*. He carried that film on his shoulders and was finally enjoying the recognition of his talents as an actor after toiling long and hard in television and trashy, light-entertainment flotsam.

For Quint, Sterling Hayden was a perfect choice. Brought up on the sea, saltwater ran in his veins and the passing years had eroded his leading-man face into a craggy, tough, weathered history of his personal ups and downs. His performance in *Dr. Strangelove* was a profoundly moving exhibition of the actor's art, and the intervening years had put a pain and character into his personality that was everything we wanted Quint to be.

It was while the casting race narrowed that I was formally put on the payroll as a screenwriter, on April 22, 1975.

On a Sunday morning, April 21, Steven called and asked if I could meet with him and Zanuck and Brown at the Bel Air. Sure. Could I come in an hour? OK. It was kind of like they didn't know where to get a writer on a Sunday when the writer stores were closed. At least it felt like that. A year later, Richard and David told me that Steven had asked for me, lobbied for me, and was given that moment to produce this wonder he had been talking about. When I first came onboard as an actor, we had discussed my writing ideas, but nothing had come of it. Now we were eleven days from start, and here we were, talking revisions. The Sunday "get acquainted" meeting turned into a six-hour discussion of the script. On Monday my agents confirmed a deal. On Tuesday, Steven and I flew to Boston and Martha's Vineyard, to start shooting a script that had not even been through its final rewrite and that was still largely uncast.

As much fun as it was to be working a definite "go" project (I had sold five screenplays already, but none had reached the screen), this was a little too close to "go" for comfort. We landed in Boston, since it was there that Steven had to finish casting the picture. Due to local Boston SAG agitation, the studio had promised to use at least ten actors from the Boston area in speaking parts,[21] and in the next few days I would begin rewriting the script under Steven's supervision, while he and Shari Rhodes (a location casting agent from Texas who had worked with him very well on *Sugarland*) walked every actor in Boston through our suite. In addition to this, I also helped deliver a Matt Hooper.

We had a three-room extravaganza of a suite in a high-rise hotel close by Boston's Combat Zone (not the racially troubled South Boston, but the red-light porno and theater district near the center of old Boston, Athens of the East). The big middle sitting room was used for casting. On one side of it was a door leading to my room, where I pounded a typewriter, emerging every now and then to stretch my legs, chat with Steven and Shari, and eyeball prospective actors as they sat across the coffee table, clutching photos and résumés in their hands. I've auditioned enough as an actor to know their discomfort, and I've produced and directed enough to learn how to ignore it. We were looking for types, and it wasn't easy. But it was required so interview we did, for three days, ten hours a day. Steven saw a lot of actors, and I got my first script revisions done.

I also called Richard Dreyfuss in New York, where he was making a personal appearance tour on behalf of *Duddy Kravitz.* Shell-shocked from being on the road in Canada, where the book is a national monument, he was on R & R at the Warwick Hotel, where I finally reached him. Now I knew Richard when he was a college sophomore, and he is, to me, a Ricky. He had been in an improvisational theater troupe called The Session in Los Angeles when I was performing at The Committee in San Francisco, and he and the other members of that company would come and visit and hang out and observe what we were doing; they were the new kids and we were the old pros. Ricky would come up with Rob Reiner (now of *All in the Family,* then a wise-kid actor/director) and Larry Bishop (then Joey Bishop's son, later an A.I.P. contract juvenile, now an actor/producer of exploitation films). Ricky had been offered the Matt Hooper part in *Jaws.* When he and Steven had met, Steven had said, "I don't want to make a film, I want to make a *movie.*" Rick liked it, then he didn't like it. Since I had this background with Rick and we had stayed friends during the intervening years, I asked him to fly up to Boston and talk about it.

He arrived spaced, with a couple of friends he'd been touring with on the road. The *Duddy Kravitz* promo junkets had given them the opportunity to continue a marathon encounter and consciousness-raising session for two straight weeks, interrupted only by room service and interviews. Consequently, Ricky's level of intensity was set quite high even for him, and the vibrations at the Boston suite got pretty zingy. (Remember, Steven was casting and watching over my shoulder as I was writing, and we were a week away from start.) So we talked.

Ricky is unhappy with the superficiality of the character. He would rather see this movie than be in it. He hates the script. It's OK, we assure him we all hate it, that's why we're fixing it, that's why Carl is here, you've got to trust us to make the changes that are necessary. Over drinks and dinner and consciousness-raising with Ricky's friends (one of whom I'd toured with on a Jane Fonda anti-war soldier show), we begin to get some mutual grasp on the character of Matt Hooper. I promise to make certain changes, Steven and Ricky agree on fundamental character traits for the part, I make notes in order to incorporate those agreements into future drafts of the script, some dialogue and business suggest themselves. And it was over room-service coffee that we discovered one of the bigger laughs in the picture, when Quint and Hooper face each other across the deck and Quint drains and crushes a beer can, throwing it over the side in one strong move, and Hooper counters by crushing a Styrofoam cup with a silly plop and putting it in a trash container onboard. We laughed then, and we laugh now. With good feelings all around, Richard goes back to New York, and his agent socks it to Universal for a whopping big chunk, and he's set for the part.[22]

Now we still didn't have a script, but we had all our principals except one. Sterling Hayden was unavailable, through no fault of his own. He wanted to do it. The studio said OK, Z and B and Steven agreed, but the U.S. government got in the way. Sterling has a tax problem, dating back to a series of unfortunate years and a succession of hostile attorneys and alimony payments. He's been living in Paris on a barge, and although he can earn money in America as a writer, through some complicated legal maneuvers which I don't understand, any income as an actor is subject to liens by the Internal Revenue Service as payment on back taxes. As a taxpayer and American citizen, Sterling is treated with the same sensitivity and care as Joe Louis. Sterling retains his dignity, makes some pictures, and gets to keep something every now and again. (Although it's reported that on one television movie he did, his take-home pay amounted to one dollar, the rest going to Uncle Sam.) So we had to look elsewhere; since Sterling's agent was not about to negotiate a huge price in order to have it all seized. Stratagems were considered, like buying a book from him for $150,000 (income as a writer, not subject to attachment), and paying him $35 a week to act in the movie. But everyone figured the IRS would see through that, so nobody tried.

Fortunately, there was another brilliant actor in the wings—the Englishman Robert Shaw. David Brown's suggestion, and an accomplished talent, he had just played the dangerous antagonist in *The Sting,* and had *The Taking of Pelham One Two Three* in the can, awaiting release. His distinguished career goes back decades, his hits are all solid gold, and he's available—for a price. He's in America finishing a limited run on Broadway and has fifty-five days left on his visa, which is more than enough to do this picture. Robert is domiciled in Ireland, not subject to any income taxes, since the Irish exempt artists from that sort of harassment, and he's happy to do the part, on a couple of conditions. The price must be right, with the proper penalties for going over-schedule. (Taxes in America are based on length of residence for an alien, and beyond a certain time, he would owe a bundle. If he could stay under the limit, he'd be home free.) We'd have to do something about his accent, which was a long way from native Yankee, and we'd have to seriously consider if we wanted him to do yet another malevolent heavy.

The problems were expensively solved, and a couple of days away from start, Robert Shaw was set as Quint, the shark killer.[23] Now, if anyone could give the shark some trouble, it would be Shaw. I still marvel at his performance in an early

James Bond epic *From Russia, with Love*. I personally found it the most entertaining of all the Bond pictures, since for the first time in his film career, 007 was faced with an opponent who looked as if he could bust Sean Connery up pretty bad. Robert has a threatening quality that is unique on the screen. Now we had a cast. And it was a good thing, too, because in three days we'd begin shooting. We left for the drive and ferry across to Martha's Vineyard. That was April 29. The show was about to start.

CHAPTER SEVEN

"Welcome to Martha's Vineyard."

(May Day 1974)

A Teamster driver from the production company came and collected us at the hotel in Boston, and an hour or so later we were eating fried clams in Woods Hole, waiting for the Nantucket and Martha's Vineyard Steamship Authority ferryboat to carry us across the narrow portion of Nantucket Sound that separated the Massachusetts mainland from the island. There's something you should understand about Martha's Vineyard. It's beautiful, picturesque, idyllic, and as unspoiled as a lot of wealthy absentee landlords can make it. There isn't a single McDonald's hamburger stand anywhere on the island, the one franchise experiment being a twelve-year-old Dairy Freeze that somehow snuck on during a nor'easter. Except for this local teenage hangout, it's all New England clapboard and redwood modern, with lots of glass, and a sprinkling of retired whaling captains' houses lining Water Street in Edgartown like a fleet of merchantmen awaiting sailing orders. There's a funky wood-frame settlement sprung up around an 1880s camp-meeting grounds, quaint little wood houses with ornate Victorian gingerbread carpenter's gothic. There are some farms and fields, some fishing villages, and some small towns, most of them incorporated in

71

the late 1600s. Lots of history, lots of tradition, lots of retired folks with money, and lots of hard-working locals trying to make an annual living out of a seasonal environment.[24] No major film had ever been shot there before, so both sides had a lot to learn. It was Hollywood meets the Yankees, and if it wasn't culture shock, it was close enough.[25]

A brief anecdote will explain the local attitude to Off–Islanders. It seems there was this Protestant couple who were anchored off Oak Bluffs, waiting to land for an annual camp meeting. The woman was pregnant, and she delivered her child aboard ship, there in the harbor. The next day, mother and child, both doing fine, were rowed ashore. They stayed on the island, and the son grew up to become one of the Vineyard's most popular ministers, living a long, full life until he passed away at age eighty-five. All during his life, except for the first few days before he was carried ashore as a babe in swaddling clothes, he never set foot off the island; when he died, he was naturally buried there. At the graveside, as he was lowered into the soil he had trod for eighty-five years, the old native islander who delivered the eulogy began with these lines: "This beloved stranger to our shores . . ." Such is the islander's feeling toward those born elsewhere. To a crew from Los Angeles, where nobody is born, it was a jolt.

On location, food and lodging are of vital concern. The workday is twelve to fourteen hours long for everyone, and the schedule runs six days a week. It's a killing pace for anyone, and for the director, who is responsible for every decision, every move, every foot of film, it poses problems greater than for others. Besides the day's shooting (which begins at 7:30 A.M.), there is exposed film from the day before to look at (the "dailies," or "rushes") and production meetings regarding the days to come. There's no time to idly decide what restaurant to go to, or even to eat an uninterrupted meal while there.

Steven had decided to ask for a house for himself, big enough for several people to share, with a full-time cook and housekeeper. An assistant to the director would live-in, and maybe the editor and the projector for dailies, to lessen the need for travel. In our case, the director's assistant was also the editor's son, which added an interesting twist to the arrangement. The house we got was an inspired choice. Five minutes from town and the production office, in Edgartown, it stood on a knoll overlooking the ocean at the end of a private road. Unlike every other house on the island, it was built as a genuine log cabin, with a forty-foot living room, and two sleeping wings, each with two bedrooms and an adjoining bath. Upstairs there was a sleeping loft, and in back a spacious lawn and a little fieldstone patio. It was adjacent to a wildlife refuge and was furnished in funky comfortable pine colonial. It was about forty years old, fully heated and weatherproofed, and made a hell of a homestead.

Ric Fields, Steven's assistant, had gone on ahead with Steve's two dogs, Elmer and Zalman,[26] and had set things up so the place was ready when we arrived. With no picture to shoot, it would have been heaven. As it was, it made life a lot more bearable in the months to come. When the dust settled, Ric was in one bedroom, I was adjoining. In the other wing, Steven had his room, with his adjoining room as a guest room. An American Film Institute observer[27] lived for a time in the loft, and the editor calculated that there wasn't enough room for her entire setup so she went to the Harbor View Hotel, where she and a few tons of equipment were settled into a two-room housekeeping apartment. I would share the house with Steven, setting my desk and typewriter up in a corner of the living room; thus I'd be able to work with his input on the script, and we'd be constantly available to each other for the ongoing development of the story. It's a nice way to work, if you don't have to shoot a picture at the same time. There was even a giant flagstone fireplace and a long refectory table for dinner. It became, simply, The Log Cabin.

While we were settling into domestic bliss, the production department was going crazy, trying to get things squared away for start of principal photography. A crew of sixty or so was arriving from California, cameras had to be checked out, generators tested, lamps and cable organized, everyone had to find quarters, an office with telephones had to be functional, and a million other details attended to. The company had a unit manager who had been on the island for weeks, securing the necessary permits, making deals for local labor and lodging, renting space to store equipment and park vehicles, and smoothing the way for the company. The local doctor's wife was our production secretary (the doctor was an Islander, with lieutenant's commissions in the Massachusetts militia signed by John Hancock hanging in his living room, handed down from generations past). She was an Off-Islander, living there twenty years married to the good doctor. Later on, he played the part of the local coroner/medical examiner. He looked the type. Doc Nevin's wife, Barbara, was a typical production secretary, as if to the manner born: quick, knowledgeable, and fond of the power of her new position, she became known to the transportation captain who shared offices with her as "Sarge."

The company had rented a house in town, installing phones and Xerox machines, radio transceivers, desks, all the paraphernalia of a battalion headquarters in the field, or a movie company on location. There was a small, tastefully lettered sign, about 24" by 36", hanging outside over the porch, stating this was the *Jaws* Production Office, a Zanuck/Brown Company, for Universal City Studios. It was a zoning violation to post a sign on that street (Edgartown is very careful about overcommercializing itself), and immediately the town's selectmen divided over the propriety of the sign, the penalties that should be leveled against the company for posting it, and whether or not to close down the office as a nonconforming use. When the poop hits the fan in Martha's Vineyard, there's no telling how far it's going to splatter.

Most of the company's initial business was finding quarters for the crew; in this respect, we became a big tourist family with a couple of million bucks to spend, arriving a little off-season. The unit manager made a deal with a local businessman who happened to own a couple of hotels, one of which was open year-round, with a dining room. A logical choice, right? Well, what we didn't know is that the businessman Bob Carroll is a self-made poor boy who came from working fishing boats and drinking pretty good up to a position of prominence that included a seat on the local board of selectmen. He owned the hotel, the bars, a local moving company, the cigarette machine franchise, and Lord knows what else. He had probably stepped on a few toes getting to where he was, and some of his fellow selectmen didn't care for Bob getting all that good fortune, so they set about making it hard for us. Which is one reason why the zoning hassle developed, and why more hassles were to plague us in the future.

And Edgartown was only one of the several townships on the island. There was Oak Bluffs, and Chilmark, and Tisbury, and West Tisbury, each with its factional disputes and family feuds going back to the days of sail. There was the traditional separation of Islanders into Up-Islanders and Down-Islanders (Edgartown was Down-Island), and the isolationists over on Chappaquiddick (the same place where Teddy Kennedy and Mary Jo Kopechne went into the water). So when you stop and take a look at it, Martha's Vineyard is like a New England house—complicated, tight, too many small rooms, hard to heat, difficult to know, and filled with prim family uncles and aunts, wary of each other's intent and suspicious of each other's loyalties. Into this baroque superstructure, the *Jaws* company came like a boisterous three-hundred-pound child, tromping on the rugs, playing with the antiques, and dripping hundred-dollar bills from its diapers.

Back in Hollywood, the shark mechanism and the accompanying sharks were loaded onto trucks for the run across the country.

We settled into our house, the crew settled into its rooms, and the unit manager started attending meetings of various town selectmen's boards and conservation commissions, scrambling to nail down the bewildering variety of permits, permissions, variances, and "we'll-look-the-other-way" accommodations that the company needed to shoot. A number of states, like Georgia, New Mexico, Arizona, Oregon, and a few others, all have film commissions, or boards, an official agency usually attached to the governor's office, whose job it is to act as high-level executive branch go-between for the film industry and local jurisdictions. But Massachusetts has no such animal, and I suspect that if it did, the governor's man would have precious little influence with the stubborn Yankees on the Vineyard. So while we above-the-line creative types struggled with the script and planned the days to come, the townies chose sides. All those who want to cooperate and make money and be in movies, over here; all those who want to keep this place unspoiled and clean and uncorrupted, over there. The cooperative faction eventually outnumbered the traditionalists, and the Universal contribution to the island's economy helped soothe ruffled feathers. But dissatisfaction, legal unpleasantness, and plain old sabotage and dirty tricks were never far away. Movies seem to bring out extremes in human behavior, and that's probably half the fun of being in the industry.

CHAPTER EIGHT

"Quiet, Please, We're Rolling."

(May 2–16, 1974)

No director likes to begin the first day of shooting with a crucial or complex scene. If something goes wrong, you're behind right from the start, and that's never any fun. *Jaws* was no exception, and the first day's filming was a simple scene. Police Chief Brody and a young college student, played by a local boy named Jonathan Filley, discover the remains of the shark's first victim, the former Chrissie. The setting is a lonely, windswept beach, the site of the previous night's beach party. In that sequence (which opens the picture and begins the story) the young man and the young woman connect, she leads him off away from the fire and plunges into the ocean for a nude swim. Too drunk to follow, he passes out on the beach, while she swims out and meets the shark, with awful consequences.

All this would be filmed later, but for now, we were concerned with the brief interrogation of the boy by Brody, the discovery of the body by a deputy, Hendricks, and a quick run up the beach to see the remains, followed by appropriate reactions to the gruesome sight. No big deal. Steven decided to do it with a long tracking shot, following the two men as they walked along a ridge above the beach, then following them as they run up the beach toward a beckoning deputy who's just caught their attention with a shrill whistle. The track took a long time to lay, but the first takes were completed before noon. With cunning and artifice and stale bread, the assistant directors had lured seagulls into the shot, and the lonely hovering birds had added a nice touch.

Jonathan Filley, the young islander from Chappaquiddick, had hung around the production, auditioned for Shari Rhodes, read for Steven, and made it on the strength of his looks, an easy, natural air, and some measure of self–confidence. He was nineteen or twenty, a student at Boston University, and he had been in a few plays at college. The extent of his self-confidence can be measured by the fact that he is even now in Hollywood, trying to pursue the career of a screen actor. As for his charm and good looks, Barbara Bass, the second assistant director out of New York, stayed in Martha's Vineyard as Jonathan's friend for four months after the picture wrapped. The beach was their first meeting. Jonathan had heard that the picture was shooting from a brother who worked at Doubleday, the book's publisher, which goes to prove that things are pretty tightly knit back East. Barbara and Jonathan are in Hollywood now, living in different apartments in the same building. She's working, he isn't. But everyone's counseled him that it takes time. By the time the picture is well into release, he will probably have an agent, photos, an answering service, and be thankful for an independent income.[28]

The first day went swimmingly, with everything finished on schedule. We wrapped around sundown and headed back to the house, to find our cook already there, bustling around the kitchen. Heaven! Location dreamland! Her name was Adele Francis. She was a born islander, and when she didn't work for us, she was employed by some of the island's grandest summer visitors—lawyers, yachtsmen, and heads of great business empires. She could cook well enough to make you cry. Her specialty was desserts of every description, and her cooking style was wholesome American with a French flair for sauces. The first day, it was kind of like having a den mother: there was Steven (26), Ric Fields (23), myself (36, the old man), the AFI observer (mid-twenties), and Rick Dreyfuss (26). I felt like the graduate student advisor to a dorm full of juniors. Adele was kind, efficient, outgoing, and I will never forget her way with a broiled lobster or a lemon cream pie. We all gained weight. Dinners around the long table became an institution, and there were rarely less than eight for dinner. On Lobster Night, when a local lobsterman favored us with twenty-five fresh caught beauties, not three hours out of the ocean, we had twenty-two folks over for dinner. Adele moaned a little, but she got dinner on for all of us. Evenings around that table were an island of harmonious sanity in what was to become a treacherous sea of shoals and setbacks.

We shot that Thursday, Friday, and Saturday. Sunday was a day off for everyone but the writer, who stayed chained to his typewriter, trying to get ahead of the schedule. Rick and Steven went skeet shooting on an island farm, guided by Alex Taylor, who lives on the island and worked as a boatman for the picture. Alex is brother to James Taylor, the musician, and Livingston Taylor, the musician, and Kate Taylor, the musician, making him one of the musical Taylor family. He was helpful to us in many ways, and we shared some high times together. The skeet blast slowed down when the beer ran out, but it was sundown by then and the rest of the shooting schedule—the film one—lay ahead.

Monday morning it began in earnest, six days a week, fourteen hours a day. If I wasn't acting, I was writing. Dinners turned into story conferences, with all the principals present, each actor discussing his part, Steven discussing the picture, me discussing the script. Adele always cleared a place next to my plate for a stenographic pad, on which I took notes as scraps of dialogue or attitudes and relationships suggested themselves. Robert Shaw arrived, along with his dear wife,

Mary Ure, who was then getting ready to appear in a play in New York. One of the tragedies of his life is her sudden death, in London in the spring of 1975. I had seen her on the stage in *Look Back in Anger* years before on Broadway, and had had a crush on her ever since. That I met her was a providential kindness. That she is gone is a cruel twist. One of my warmest memories of the Vineyard is their sparkling wit, their charm, and evenings spent at the Log Cabin and at the house they rented, a few miles away, also on the water.

Mary and Robert had a manservant with them, an elegant Robert Morley type, Eric Harrison. He and Mary and Robert had just arrived on the island when they got a taste of New England hospitality. A local eccentric fired a few rifle bullets through their front door, penetrating the walls and chipping tile as they ricocheted around the downstairs bath. The local thought the house was empty. He never explained why he fired shots into it. The incident was kept quiet, but there is nothing like a jacketed bullet from a deer rifle whizzing through the house to make a person wonder if he's in the right place. Fortunately, no one was standing in the wrong place. It was Eric, flouncing out of the guest cottage in his robe and slippers (the shots were fired late at night), who first looked at the fresh hole in the door and said, "I believe they're shooting, sir." Soon afterward, Mary returned to New York to do a play; Eric tended to Robert's needs, appearing on the set with a thermos flask of hot English tea; and the eccentric with the rifle was fined and released.

Dinners continued as before, with Shaw, Scheider, Dreyfuss, Lorraine Gary, Steven, Verna Fields, and myself spending most of the time discussing the script. Adele would bring in the main course, or the dessert and coffee, we'd spend the usual ten minutes in extravagant praise (never undeserved), and then return to the script. Everybody would leave around 9:30 P.M., Steven would go to bed at 10:00, and I'd keep a lonely vigil at the typewriter, tapping on into the night, reducing the dinner-table information exchange into a passable script. At dawn, Steven would stumble out of bed to read last night's pages over a cup of hot tea, and I'd wake up the script typist with an early morning call, pass the pages through Zanuck/Brown, and pedal my bicycle over to the production office to meet her. She'd type the material into clean pages, which would be copied and distributed to the department heads and actors and script supervisor on the set at 8 A.M. Other days, when I wasn't writing up against the gun, I'd just hand the new pages to her during the day, and she'd have a couple of days to get them out. The pressure wasn't constant, but it never dropped to a manageable level.

Knowledgeable movie makers reading this will shudder over the process I've just described, so let me explain why. In any film, especially a big-budget theatrical feature, the script is a crucial road map and guide to every physical production department. The cameraman must know what he is going to be asked to shoot. The production manager has to know where, and how many actors will be required. The prop man wants to have his props ready, the wardrobe department wants to know whose clothes to lay out, and so on down the line. The script is a bible, and on the set, when money is disappearing down the tubes at about $3,000 an hour, a twenty-minute wait for the prop man to go get some beer that was not indicated in his pages costs the company a grand. All it takes is a few of these moments a day for a couple of weeks and all of a sudden the picture is days over schedule and hundreds of thousands of dollars over budget. So nobody likes surprises. And surprises were emerging with every revision. "No coast guard station, boys, we've cut that scene." Out the window go weeks of getting permission to shoot, the rental of coast guard uniforms, and all the collateral work of preparing that scene. And, "The scene on the beach will be with all the extras." Out go the phone calls to eighty-five locals to show up at some corner of the island. These changes were never arbitrary or capricious; they were integral to the revised story that was emerging as fast as I could rewrite. But a certain desperation began to creep into the production department as they received each set of changes, their bloodshot eyes feverishly dancing down the pages, looking for new details, new effects, changes that would make their work tougher, their hours longer, their tempers shorter. "Admit it," someone asked me a week into the picture. "You guys are making it up as you go along." We weren't, but it must have felt that way to the production guys.

But the above-the-line creatives weren't the only ones throwing monkey wrenches. The Up-Island Vineyarders had their own view of the world, and for a time, *Jaws* didn't fit into it. Joe Alves had designed a home for Quint, the fisherman, that was a masterpiece of a set. Multileveled, it reeked of blood and fish guts, was dressed with a marvelous collection of eccentric props and furniture, and was a perfect visualization of the complex character that Robert was playing. In the "final" version of the script that everyone had recklessly assumed would be the last, several important scenes were to be played in different areas of that set, so Joe had conceived this thirty-eight-foot-high shed, with a work area, a living floor, a sleeping loft, and adjacent anchorage for Quint's boat, the *Orca*, and a dock connecting it all. The ideal location had been found, in the insufferably quaint fishing village of Menemsha, Up-Island out Tisbury way. You've seen the town on countless postcards, and there's a bar named after it on Fifty-Seventh Street in New York, where a miniature diorama of Menemsha goes through a little thunderstorm every hour, and you can watch the harbor lights blink on and off in time to the alcohol beating in your brain. Menemsha had a vacant lot right in the middle of it, owned by a Down-Island chap who rented it to the company. The building was a set, as we've pointed out. It was to be erected, filmed in, and removed. It had removable walls, to allow the camera to peer in from convenient angles, and it was, as I say, a picturesque and charming structure. It was also thirty-eight-feet high, and Menemsha has a twenty-four-foot height limit in their building code.

The first thing the Menemsha locals want is that the thing be built according to the local construction code. Now Hollywood is prepared to spend money, but it's not prepared to lay a concrete foundation, put studs on 16" centers, double-sheath the walls and flooring, and put all electrical connections in metal conduit, and connect sewage and waste lines for a set that will be used for six days and scrapped. "Well then," say the locals. "How do we know you'll take it down when you're done?" "Because we always do," comes the reply, quick as a flash. "In that case, you can just post a bond," say the Menemsha smart guys, and Universal has to go through the hassle of putting $100,000 in a Boston bank to guarantee its restoration of the scenic Menemsha waterfront to its pristine state. Universal further agrees to pay the town $1,000 a day for every day past June 15 that the set is left standing. Talk about cooperation with the locals!

Finally, the building permits are all obtained, local variances granted, and Joe Alves is there to supervise the driving of the few piles that will support the structure while it's up. As he's standing there with his blueprints and drawings, making gestures with his foot to "Start here," there's a tap on his shoulder, and a new, strange face appears. "You're driving a pile below the mean high water mark." "That's right," says Joe. "You got a permit?" Joe produces about a thousand square yards of paperwork, none of which is what the gentleman wants. It seems that everybody's jurisdiction runs out at the waterline, and since this one pile is going to be driven into about six inches of water, it's a matter for the Commonwealth of Massachusetts, and Universal needs a special permit from the state. "How long does that take?" Joe asks. "Six months, if it's a rush job," answers the man. Now we've got problems, so Joe inquires further. "What if we put this thing up without a permit?" "You'll just be ordered to tear it down, fella." "How long does that take?" "About six weeks, buddy. They move fast on that kind of violation." "Done!" says Joe with a happy smile, and the piles get driven and the thing gets built.

In the rewrite, the scenes in Quint's shack dwindle away, until there's only one brief encounter played there, but Steven spends a few days shooting it, the camera shows most of it, and everyone's happy, especially the local folks who now like this beautiful set so much they want to leave it standing as a tourist attraction, until the officials remind them that there's a bond requiring it to be disassembled upon completion of shooting there. "Can't we leave it up?" "No." Especially since this poor vacant lot is vacant for a reason. Like I said, it belongs to some Down-Islander whom nobody Up-Island seems to fancy, and for the past fifteen years or so, as long as he's owned this particular piece of choice Menemsha waterfront, they've been denying him a building permit of any kind. Getting Quint's shack up was just a tease, I suppose. That spot next to the general store and post office in Menemsha is a little parking lot again, and will probably stay that way until the poor guy who owns it either sells it, or (knowing the Menemsha locals) until he promises to put up a $100,000 bond guaranteeing he'll tear down whatever it is they give him permission to build.

Shooting goes on. We are filming a scene in which Brody and Hooper, accompanied by Meadows, are at sea in a small boat, looking for evidence of a great white shark. The script calls for them to find the wrecked hull of a local fisherman's boat. They tie up alongside it, closer examination shows terrible damage, Hooper puts on a wet suit and dives to inspect its hull, and pries the tooth of a villainous shark out of the hull. Dramatic stuff, but in an agonizing story session, I later concede that there's no reason for me, "Meadows," to be in the scene, and Steven insists it would be spookier to play it at night with just Brody and Hooper. But all this is after the fact. The reality is that we are two miles out in Nantucket Sound, bordering the Atlantic Ocean, in a dreadfully overloaded small boat. Besides us three principals, there's a technical advisor to run the boat, Steven the director, a cameraman, a camera operator, a sound recordist, a script supervisor, and a grip. Sitting in the hold are about a thousand pounds of batteries to power the portable lighting we're using. We're riding low in the water.

We shoot the dialogue for a while, the cameraman moving around to various setups, balancing the forty-pound Panaflex camera on his shoulder, trying not to fall into the ocean every time the boat hits a wave. We're acting away like crazy, and soon it's time to get a shot of us pulling up alongside the wrecked boat. This is a long shot, so the camera is moved to the relative stability of an anchored barge, with a support boat standing by and a fast speedboat to run back and forth, carrying instructions from Steven (or Steven himself). We rehearse it a few times, then we're left alone to make the approach. Rick Dreyfuss, who has never been on a boat before this picture, is at the helm. Roy Scheider, following the script, is clinging to the aft transom, being seasick and tired. I (wearing my "actor" cap today) am pretending to lean over to grab a rope and tie us up as we pull alongside. Fred Zendar, our technical advisor, is huddled out of sight below the gunwale, actually steering the boat and throttling the engine while Rick makes believe he's an oceanographer with years of small-boat handling experience. Except for Roy, we're all acting like crazy. He's seated next to a couple of barrels of real dead fish heads, which the prop man has obligingly placed onboard to serve as "chum" (a kind of shark bait), so he doesn't have to act too much to be sick and tired. On the third take, we are pulling alongside as usual, but the Zendar/Dreyfuss navigational team is a little off, so the gap between the two boats is more than I'm used to. I lean out, try to grasp the rope, lean further, and feel a new sensation—that of knowing I am about to plunge headlong into the icy sea. I feel my center of gravity pass the point of no return, and, graceful as you please, it's headfirst into the ocean.

"Cut!" Freddy Zendar saves my life by pulling the key out of the ignition, stopping the propellers from chewing my body into extra parts. I save my life by treading water like a man possessed, buoyed up by adrenalin surge and plain anxiety. I'm wearing two sets of long underwear under my costume, which is supposed to indicate a midsummer day, when it's actually late spring and very cold out there, with a four-foot swell, winds from the north, and no warming current to heat up the water. I'm bobbing around telling everyone to keep calm, I'm OK, and trying to direct my rescue. Over on the camera barge they're dithering, and inside the small boat Fred Zendar is scrambling to find the diving ladder to put over the side to give me a foothold so I can climb out of the water. He knows, and I remember, that in water as cold as Nantucket Sound, twenty minutes is about all you've got before hypothermia and shock render you incapable of movement and you drown. (It's only about 48°–52° in there, I find out later.)

All the while I'm kicking and saying, "Don't panic, just get the ladder, I'm OK," and other reassuring exclamations. I think about sharks in the water, and dismiss that as an impossible jest. About that, at least, I'm right. Nothing nibbles my toes. Fred gets the ladder over the side, and I'm pulled aboard in record time. The speedboat picks me up and takes me to the support boat, a smelly local fishing boat rented by the company. The rest of the company is standing there excited, radio reports of my dip have alerted the production office, but after some hot soup and a change into dry clothes (thoughtfully provided by the wardrobe department "just in case") we go on to film the rest of the scene. Total delay in shooting, a half-hour or so. Later in the afternoon, as we're shooting more dialogue, Steven directs us to head into the waves, because the camera isn't getting enough splashing to give a sense of being at sea. Fred Zendar shakes his head, but puts us about, and as we're playing the next take, I hear the cameraman go "Ooops!" as a wave almost sweeps him over the side. The swell crashes over the bow, dropping about a hundred gallons of seawater onto the sound recorder, who takes a wet earphone out of his head and comments, "That's a wrap for sound." Cold, drenched in spray, seasick, and thoroughly uncomfortable, we head back in. And that was our first day shooting on the ocean. One soaked principal, one change of wardrobe, and a $2,500 Nagra recorder shot. Neptune was trying to tell us something.

Without trying to get the scene, we agreed later to shoot it over as a night sequence, and that was that for Meadows at sea.[29] Over on the other side of the point, a bunch of trucks pulled up with Bob Mattey and his very special cargo. The shark was here.

CHAPTER NINE

"Bruce, the Shark."

(May 17–June 1, 1974)

Whatever their other talents, production crews are not noted for their satiric taste or sophisticated humor; under severe pressure, they will come up with gems, but given time to think about it, their jokes run to the obvious. A time-honored classic in the industry (very clever the first time out, about fifty years ago) is to call to a brother crew member who's standing in range of the camera when a take is about to roll, "Lick your lips!" (a reminder to look moist and dewy-lipped for the camera; it's something models and actresses do, and hairy grips and electricians don't). Ho ho and ho again. So it was inevitable that of all the names in the world for the monster shark, the boys in the shop would love "Bruce." In fact, he was named after Steven's attorney.[30] To everyone's credit, once we were in production, the shark was more often referred to as "that sonofabitchin' bastard rig," or something equally direct. As much as I've told you about Bruce up to now could have gotten me a severe reprimand and maybe even a dismissal during the filming. The only reason this is being written now is because the book will be released a little after the movie, and many of you will have already seen what we're talking about so the mystery won't be destroyed for you if we tell you a little bit about how it was done.[31]

Steven, Richard Zanuck, and David Brown all thoroughly agreed on at least one thing—the shark was to remain a mystery. There was to be no press about the elaborate mechanical models that were to be used, and certainly no pictures of the great beasts as they hung lifeless in their cradles, or were towed patiently out to sea in their special barge. A guard was summarily fired when an enterprising reporter for the *Christian Science Monitor* snuck into the boat shed where the sharks were kept and took pictures. We all believed that an audience's enjoyment of the picture would be severely diminished if they had read for months in advance about how the shark was just a mechanical contraption. Audiences being what they are, we felt sure they'd be thousands of wise guys pointing to the screen, saying, "Look, you can see it's not real—there's the machinery, there's the operator, hiding inside. See how it's up out of the water? No real shark would do that," thereby thoroughly destroying the illusion for that happy majority that has willingly suspended its disbelief in order to enjoy the story at the moment. Half the time they would be wrong, pointing like yahoos to real sharks filmed at considerable risk, exclaiming, "Look, it's phony!"

When the picture was finally edited, dubbed, and scored, it was shown to Ron and Valerie Taylor, the world's leading experts in photographing the great white shark, and, indeed, the camerapersons who had recorded our own second-unit footage in Australia. They couldn't tell their own footage from ours, so perfectly did everything match. It was only when they saw Bruce in action with the principals that they could be sure what was theirs and what wasn't. So if your smart buddy, or your own smart self, wants to go back and look at the movie to pick out the mechanical shark shots, good luck, and remember people almost got killed making it look real for you. If you want to get tough about it, most everything that's ever thrilled or delighted you in the movies has been an illusion of some sort. A lot of *The Exorcist*'s magic is gone when you repeat to yourself "Campbell's Split Pea Soup" during the spit-up scenes. And nobody really got killed in *The Godfather*, you know, so don't be like some folks and insist on knowing how everything is done. I'll tell you, but try and be cool about it, and when you see the picture after reading this, relax and watch the clouds in the background, if you have to watch something other than the action and emotion.

With these cautions out of the way, I will now describe some of the mechanics of shark operation, some of the frenzies they caused, and how everyone related to the great whites we had on Martha's Vineyard. You will have to hunt pretty far for any photos of phony sharks, however—the still department's choices of shark pictures have been deliberately kept confusing, and you won't see any mechanisms anywhere.

Special effects are called "gags," and when James Caan is splattered with a hundred machine-gun bullets, that's called a gag. (Like in a joke, not like in choke.) A major special effect (the destruction of Los Angeles, say) is a series of gags: i.e., the chandelier-fall gag, the ground-opening-up gag, etc.

Bob Mattey, the special effects wizard, had devised a number of shark gags, conceived by Steven, made into visual continuity by Joe Alves, built and operated by Bob Mattey's crew, supervised by Bob or another special effects man if Bob was busy. Bob was busy a lot, working in an area where we had rented a fenced shed and boat landing and some spare property, in order to erect the East Coast edition of Shark City. Shark City was where the sharks were built, over at Rolly Harper's lot in Los Angeles's San Fernando Valley, and when they had been shipped to the Vineyard it became appropriate to call their new home Shark City, too. (Rolly Harper's catering trucks were there as well, feeding our cast and crew.) Shark City included a shed to house the equipment; space to tie up the floating barge that held the air compressors, tanks and related tools and equipment to operate and maintain the beasts; and all the material that was necessary to support the sharks at sea: coils of pneumatic hose, welding tanks, torches, ropes, generators, extra structural steel, ballast tanks, copper, iron, steel, plastic, electrical motors, pneumatic motors, and hydraulic rams. It was a real gadget-lover's paradise. There was a floating cradle for the shark itself, with a ramshackle wooden superstructure on which hung flapping tarpaulins and sheets of plastic to hide the monster from prying eyes. The special effects crew felt they had enough to do without serving as security guards too, so screening the shark from tourists became a sometime thing. But there it all was, quietly attracting flies and attention.

All during the first weeks of filming, the shark was being hastily made ready so that it would work when it was called. Unfortunately, due to the press of the schedule and the brisk start, Bruce had never been tested in ocean water. There had been a few partial tests of paint and rubber, but nothing definitive, like plunging the whole creature into the ocean. Since Joe and his painter, Ward Welton, were in Martha's Vineyard when the sharks were completed, the fish were shipped unpainted, with a creamy yellow neoprene plastic exterior. There were, all told, three full-scale models of the twenty-five-foot great white. Each one was made of welded tubular steel, with flexible joints hinging moving sections. The tail swung from side to side, the sides rolled, the fins waved: the models moved like real sharks. One was entirely open on the left side, one was open on the right side, and one was solid and complete. The open ones would always present their complete side to the camera, and would be attached to the steel platform sunk on the bottom of the ocean, riding the trolley along specially greased rails, simulating swimming action. They could dive, surface, look to camera, bite, snarl, chew, flop their tails, and carry on most realistically for sixty or seventy feet of travel. The closed shark was attached to a "sea sled," a complicated submerged mechanism consisting of rudder planes and bracing, like a skeletal submarine. This baby could maneuver freely along the surface, guided by scuba divers with oxygen tanks riding the sled around below the waves, working the fins and planes.

Each shark weighed about 2,000 pounds complete and had an internal welded steel skeleton, over which was fastened "flesh" made of neoprene foam with closed cells (nonabsorbent), over which was a polyurethane skin reinforced with nylon stretch material at the flexible joints. Inside, fastened to the skeletal armature, were twenty or thirty pneumatic rams and motors to drive the moving parts: lashing the tail, opening and closing the mouth, rolling the eyes, and the like. It was designed to be of neutral weight in the water, but with the pneumatic mechanisms there was a constant ebb and flow of compressed air, changing the underwater dynamics constantly. In addition, some of the plastics would absorb water after a few hours of submersion, so the shark would put on about 10 or 12 percent of its own weight with every outing. The one-sided sharks were no problem for flotation, since they could equalize pressure immediately through the open side. The sea-sled shark was trickier, and it was vented through the tail and the belly, where the rush of bubbles would be invisible in the wake and turbulence of its movement.

The skin was a special problem. There is no known substance that has the elasticity and flexibility of real flesh and skin, so the art department had to invent it. There were a few special formula paints that formed a rubbery surface when dry, and these were made up to specifications and applied. No good! Real sharkskin has a sandpapery texture all its own, like a cat's tongue. Running your hand along a shark from nose to tail, it's smooth and sleek and hydrodynamic. Run your hand the reverse way, and you'll scrape it raw on the tough-textured skin. In the South Seas, local boatbuilders use shark's skin as sandpaper, working on Philippine mahogany with it. Our sharks had a polyurethane skin, which when painted took on the sheen of a plastic model slot car. No good. Joe and Ward discovered that #40 silica (sandblasting sand) added to the paint with a separate blower would blend to give the skin a texture and feel not unlike the real thing. Water wouldn't bead on it unrealistically, and it would catch the light like a flesh surface, and not like an artificial one. So there they stood, two paint-spray blowers in hand, applying $30 per gallon special paint with one hand and sand with the other, all in the name of art. The paint itself had a brief shelf life and would self-destruct three weeks after formulation at the factory, so it was flown from California to Martha's Vineyard in the Universal pouch, along with the dailies and executive correspondence. Later, during an emergency, Ward had to patch a rough spot at sea and discovered that a $1.98 can of spray paint and a handful of #40 silica would give the same effect over small areas. And once, underwater, Ward took an instant scuba lesson (he had never dived before), borrowed some Pan Stick (actor's greasepaint) from the makeup man, and gave the shark an instant touch-up, underwater. When the clock is on and the film is shooting, time and money must be saved, and there's no limit to the ingenuity and inventiveness of a pressured crew.

But all the ingenuity in the world can't fight physical fact, and the first crisis point was the failure of the paint to stick to the new sharks. Panic! Tests had been conducted in California, but on Martha's Vineyard the temperature and humidity were all different, and adjustments had to be made. And they were, and work went on. We were shooting away, slowly completing those pages in which the actors acted with each other on land, relentlessly approaching the day when there'd be nothing left to shoot but the shark. Work went on feverishly at Shark City, and Richard Zanuck and David Brown carefully stayed away, not wishing to see anything less than perfection, being as how this entire project rested on the believability and workability of these never-been-done-before machines. Bob Mattey enthusiastically reported fair progress on the fishes; Dick and David were satisfied, Steven curious. "How's the shark coming?" "Be ready when you are." "Let's hope so." But before the big babies could be tested there was a live shark crisis to contend with.

CHAPTER TEN

"Teddy, We Got to Have a Shark by Monday."

(June 2–10, 1974)

In the script, there's a scene in which the distraught mother of the second victim posts a reward for the shark that killed her son. It's a $3,000 bounty, and in the evening, two men anxious to get a jump on the rest of the island try to catch the shark with a hook and chain anchored to a pier, baited with a holiday roast, with an old inner tube for a float. Both actors were locals, one of them from Boston SAG, the other a guy off the Vineyard.[32] Casting them had been a problem, with Shari constantly approaching Steven during shooting and begging him to make up his mind and set someone, anyone, to play these two bozos. The decision was put off a number of times, under the pressure of competing problems, each demanding the director's fullest attention. Finally, with only days to go before the sequence, Steven set the parts. The special effects crew had built a breakaway pier and rigged the gag so one man would go into the water and the other guy stay on the pier.[33] The story calls for the chain and bait to be taken by some massive force which pulls the dock apart, dumping one of the greedy bounty hunters into the drink. The fragment of dock is towed out to sea, then makes an abrupt turn, and starts after the man. The man alternated between dying and surviving in various editions of the script; in the final version, we elected to play the scene for the terror of being in the ocean with the unseen monster. We'd then cut to the next morning, by which time news of the bounty would be all over New England and Police Chief Brody's jurisdiction would be flooded with would-be shark hunters determined to win the money for themselves.

The scene was shot day for night, which meant difficult work for the cameraman, who would have to photograph several successive days of widely varying sun and skies to look as if it were the same predawn darkness. To further complicate things, it blew up rainy fog, which meant sometimes you could see the ocean and pier, and other times you couldn't. Looking for angles that would satisfy the director, the story, the cameraman, and at the same time avoid problems of lighting or background was difficult and demanding work. Much of the scene was shot from out in the water, which meant that grips and gaffers would have to work in deep water, stringing 10,000-watt arc lights, finding a stable camera platform in shifting sandy bottom, or shooting from the water level itself, with the camera in a water-tight box. The clumsiness and inexperience of the two actors did not make the work go any faster. Although sincere in their efforts, they seemed unable to get things right, and the sequence went on, take after take after take. Finally, it came time to do the breakaway pier gag. Underwater cables were rigged, timbers sawn through partway, everything set. At this point, as is customary, Steven asked both men if they'd want a stand-in or stunt double for the difficult moment when the pier breaks and one scrambles to safety while the other goes into the drink. SAG requires an actor be given the opportunity of using a stunt man for anything that looks even remotely dangerous or injurious. Most experienced pros step back and let the stunt man do the dangerous work. That's what they're paid for, and a twisted ankle or scraped forehead is OK, if not exactly desirable. The professional would just as soon not risk his agility or attractive features in a stunt that could easily be doubled. (In cases where the switch would be obviously a cheat, many performers, including stars, would rather attempt the stunt themselves, so that the continuity of the shot can be preserved without cutting away or editing around the moment when the stunt man is substituted. Witness Genevieve Bujold in *Earthquake*, standing on a hill while real, heavy, dangerous objects tumble by on either side of her.) But our two boys elected to do it all themselves. So into the water they went, one swimming, the other scrambling up. So far, so good. The next day, it was time to get the shots of the man swimming, and scrambling up the broken pier. Over and over and over we did it, Steven calling for take after take. Months later, when we talked about that scene, he confessed that it was an unconscious urge to punish that drove him to seek perfection in the takes. Had he realized it then he might not have striven for such perfection, and the actor who went into the drink might have spent fewer hours in a rubber wet suit with full street clothes on top of it, pretending to swim for his life, choking on salt water, breaking his nails on the rough boards of the dock, and puffing his way through a dozen different angles of the scene.

To be fair, I should point out that Steven and the crew were also in wet suits, and spent as long, if not longer, in the icy waters trying to get the shot as the man spent trying to do it right. Almost a year later, when the picture was completed, the voices of both actors were completely replaced on the soundtrack, redubbed on a soundstage by Hollywood actors with water in their mouths. The scene had such a jinx on it, even this had to be redone, with a third set of actors replacing the voices of the second set of actors who replaced the voices of the original set of actors. It was one of those sequences that never go right. (There's one of them in every film, if you're lucky. If you're unlucky, you can get a whole picture that never goes right.) And when I say a sequence or bit goes right, I'm speaking of a subjective judgment by the director and editor, who are always keenly aware of technical errors that the audience in the theater never sees, moments that pass in an instant, mistakes so adroitly covered that even other professionals have difficulty in spotting them. But once you know where the fluff is, and stare at it for eight months of editing and postproduction, it never fails to jump off the screen at you every time the picture's screened.

The Pier Scene, as we called it, plays quite nicely now; audiences laugh in the right places, the suspense is good, and the damned pier finally makes a correct turn to come back in pursuit of the chump in the water. For months, it didn't. Teddy Grossman, an old friend of Dick Zanuck's and a gifted stunt man, watched the whole thing as it was shot, sipping coffee and waiting to see if he'd be called upon to take the fall. He never was. Teddy was required for a far more important chore.

As a result of the bounty posted for the shark there's a comic-opera armada of sane and insane sailors who go out in all varieties of fishing gear and try to hook the monster fish. Most of their antics wound up on the floor, but there's a hint of what their action was still in the picture. In any event, they return to shore with a thirteen-foot tiger shark, believing this awesome animal to be the one that killed the little Kintner boy, thereby qualifying for the bounty. They've all had a hand in killing it: the big fish has been hooked, shot, clubbed, stabbed, even pierced with hunting arrows. It's hung up on the dock, pictures taken to circulate in the press to assure people that Amity has eliminated its problem, and only the young ichthyologist, Hooper, remains unconvinced. The Armada Scene is a complex flurry of movement and action, culminating with the appearance of Mrs. Kintner, the bereaved mother, who slaps Brody's face and publicly accuses him of knowingly participating in the cover-up of the death of the shark's first victim, Brody thereby carrying some of the responsibility for her boy's death. We had been assured that there was no shortage of big sharks in the Atlantic waters off Martha's Vineyard and that one could be caught in time for the scene on the dock with the armada. A couple of local fishermen who bragged of their experience had been engaged, and they had set off weeks before in search of a big shark that could be hung up on the pier to look as if it might have killed the Kintner boy. All the while we had been shooting other scenes, the sequence on the dock with the fish was drawing closer. All we got from the local pros was radio reports of bad weather, and promises to do better tomorrow.

Eventually, the big-time shark hunters we had hired turned up with a few blues, about a foot across and eight or nine feet long; they were ordinary sharks, capable of taking off an arm or leg, but not normally hostile to man and certainly not menacing enough to fool anyone as being the killer of the little boy. The scene with the dead shark was due to shoot Monday. On Thursday before, it was apparent that the deadline was growing near and there was no shark. There wasn't time to build a good one, every bit of the art department's skill was required in getting the main shark ready, as well as making a duplicate of the *Orca* (Quint's boat) that would sink on cue.

Teddy Grossman has a friend who's the director of player personnel for the Miami Dolphins, so he calls him in Florida to see if they got any sharks down there this time of year. "Yeah, we got sharks—somebody left a dead nine-footer in front of the bar last night" comes the response. The head of casting at Universal, back in the Tower in Hollywood, has contracts with some sports fishermen in Sarasota and they guarantee a shark that's like the one we need. So Teddy and Fred Zendar, the Ancient Mariner, fly down to Miami and Sarasota to catch a shark.

Fred Zendar is a Swiss gentleman who left his native Alps to be a newsreel cameraman in the 1920s. He was on the Long

March with Mao in China, he was with Hemingway in Cuba, he was with Spencer Tracy as technical advisor on *The Old Man and the Sea*. He's worked on hundreds of sea pictures at all the studios, and he has master's papers entitling him to steer anything short of a 100 tons displacement, all oceans, or something like that. He lives near the ocean in Santa Monica, California, and at this writing he is down in Mexico with the crew of *Lucky Lady*, working on a colossal sea battle of 1920s rum-runners and coast guardsmen. I hear they're shooting on the water, in the actual ocean, with real boats. I also hear they're way behind schedule. We could've told them.

Anyway, there they are in Sarasota, Florida: the Ancient Mariner and lively Teddy Grossman, carrying a couple of thousand of Universal's dollars with them, trying to be un-obtrusive in a beach community that looks like it's a cross between *Deliverance* and *The Land That Time Forgot*. These big old local boys decide they will do the job and get the shark, so Saturday morning, out they go. Fred and Teddy are pacing the sand, knowing that the shark works Monday, and that if they don't come up with it, they might as well not go back. But by nightfall the good ol' boys are back with a perfect specimen: a thirteen-foot tiger shark, a man-eater, the right size and everything, killed clean with a single twelve-gauge shotgun blast from a Powerhead, right on top between the eyes. Nice going. Only the price has changed. The good ol' boys want more money, and there's a little waterfront haggling going on, Teddy trying to keep his pockets straight—this one's got the airfare, this is his per diem, this is for the loot for the shark. The deal is struck, and now our boys are the proud possessors of a 750-pound dead shark, and it's Saturday night. Obviously, he's not going back to the motel with them. So they truck him overland to a freezer locker used by the local sports fishers, and stash him until morning. They also contract with the boys to build a crate for the beast, and then they scurry around buying up a lot of rock salt and ice to pack the fish for the long trip home.

By now it's becoming apparent that there's no commercial airline that wants to take a fifteen-foot wooden casket containing the recently demised corpse of a 750-pound shark as carry-on luggage, or even as a checked bag, or airfreight, or anything. And it doesn't matter that the fish is wrapped in plastic and doesn't leak. Dead sharks start to get ripe very quickly, due to the extremely simple nature of their proteins. They're primitive life forms, no skeletons, just cartilage, and they spoil even faster than regular fish, and you know how they go, right? So Fred calls home and says, "We got the fish, only we can't get him back in time," while Teddy goes to look for whoever it was who last had the key to the ice locker.

Bill Gilmore, never one to cut corners in a pinch, immediately dispatches a private jet that can handle the load. The jet will be in Sarasota at 1 P.M. They find the fella with the key, and the shark is given its final packing: ice, rock salt, and a case of open Airwick from the local market. The top of the wooden casket is nailed down, and the sides lettered with picturesque slogans: "Zendar/Grossman Shark Hunters," "Call Me Oscar," and the like. The jet arrives, the fish-in-the-box is at the airport, only there's no forklift. It's Sunday, and the operator has gone fishing. So everybody—Fred, Teddy, the ol' boys, even the pilot—physically hump the giant crate with the 1,200 pounds of dead shark and ice and Airwick and plastic into the plane. The final kicker is there's no room for two passengers plus the shark, so Fred, a key man, flies back with the stinky fish pack, and Teddy goes home via commercial, out of Miami.

Monday morning, in front of about 250 cast and crew, the crate is pried open, and the big shark is hung on its mark. It's ripe at dawn, and by noon there's a big empty place in the crowd downwind of it whenever the camera's not actually rolling. I'm acting in this scene, but fortunately my part calls for me to stand at a distance and call directions to the crowd, asking the armada bounty hunters that caught the shark to

102 • Carl Gottlieb

pose with it for the papers, so we can spread the news to the world that the killer is caught. With the complicated exposition, a little cross-talk between Rick and Roy, a brief exchange with Murray Hamilton, and the difficult slap and speech by the island woman playing Mrs. Kintner,[34] the scene takes about four days to shoot. Every day is worse than the one preceding. The makeup man has been called in to freshen up the dead shark, and the first attempts make our extravagantly purchased real dead prop look like a cheap rubber mock-up. So makeup tries again, and it gets better, but the shark has got a bad case of jet lag and wet rot, and in the position it's in, what with the mouth pulled open and all, anyone standing close can look into its gullet and see the guts of it piling up in the throat, getting ready to spill onto the deck in a very messy way. Fortunately, the horror-on-a-hook is finally cut down, and we wrap the sequence.[35] Everybody figures we're through with shark meat for a while, but a week or so later some local anonymous joker leaves a brown shark on the steps of the production office. Quaint Vineyard humor.

CHAPTER ELEVEN

"How Far Along Are We?"

(June 11–20, 1974)

The merry month of May passed as we continued to film the land portions of the picture. At nights, I was rewriting; during the days, acting, waiting to act, watching others act, or writing. The script was moving faster than the picture, which was fine. If it had been the other way around, we would've been standing around with nothing to shoot but obsolete pages.

Jaws was further blessed by the presence of its editor, a woman affectionately referred to in *Newsweek* as "Mother Cutter." She was Verna Fields,[36] another veteran of the industry, a daughter of a great MGM contract writer, Sam Hellman, whose credits include *Little Miss Marker* for Shirley Temple. Verna had begun her apprenticeship thirty years ago on a Fritz Lang film and worked her way up the editorial ladder as a sound cutter, assistant editor, and then full editor, stopping along the way to teach at the University of Southern California's film department and produce a series of films for the government. In the last few years she's been the editor of *American Graffiti, Paper Moon, Daisy Miller,* and *What's Up, Doc?* She had met Steven when she collaborated on the editing of *Sugarland Express.* Verna came to dinner almost every night and relieved me (reluctantly) of the responsibility of being Senior Faculty Advisor at the Log Cabin.

Many films are edited after-the-fact, upon completion of principal photography, with an assistant editor performing the routine chores of matching picture and sound on the dailies and coding all the printed takes. Verna is one of those who insists, if it's at all possible, on being present for the entire filming of a picture, on location or at home, and working in close collaboration with the director. She had worked this way with Steven before on *Sugarland*, when the postproduction proceedings had been conducted at her pleasant little house on a modest street in Van Nuys. Steven enjoys close supervision of editing and is one of a breed of filmmakers who must see every edit, collaborate on every cut, and live with a picture from the initial planning through the final release print.

Verna's presence on the Vineyard was an extension of this close collaboration and a thorough involvement of almost all the creative forces in a simultaneous expression of abilities. Writer, director, actors, producers, editor, all present for cross-fertilization of ideas and internal testing of approaches. Under Steven's supervision, and Dick and David's benevolent (but worried) eye, the picture continued to grow. Verna, working at all hours in her room, was able to rough-cut together whole sequences as they were filmed, and often we'd be able to look at a scene just a few days after it was shot, seeing in it an approximation of its final form, as it would look in the completed movie. We would see if characters were working, if exposition had been laid out, excitement provided, tension established, all that creative hoo-hah that filmmakers often wait for until the picture is through shooting, when it's too late to undo mistakes without expensive retakes which are often impossible or prohibitively expensive. Perpetually on a diet, Verna would sometimes get up past midnight and resist the impulse to snack by cutting a scene.

The production board, with its all-important strips of cardboard, had been violently rearranged. The original plan had called for a number of beach sequences to be shot early in May. As it turns out, Martha's Vineyard and Cape Cod depend on a seasonal shift of the Gulf Stream current to warm their waters for swimming and recreation. This shift occurs late in May and early in June, and the water isn't really comfortable until July 4. But that fact hadn't been thoroughly appreciated early in the scheduling. It wasn't until the company was on the island that it became painfully clear that no local resident would attempt to go swimming before mid-June (except for a few crazies and members of the Polar Bear Club).

The beach sequences were Panic Scenes; the first one an off-season one, just before the Fourth of July weekend, when the residents of Amity enjoy their uncrowded beaches for the last time before the summer influx of tourists. The second beach sequence takes place on the Fourth of July weekend, after Police Chief Brody has been thwarted in his desires to close the town's public beaches for fear of the great white shark. Both sequences required large numbers of swimmers to be seen in the water in order to succeed.

No extras to go in the water meant no possible way of shooting these sequences in a realistic manner (although there was some talk of outfitting stuntmen in flesh-colored wet suits and having them pretend to be summer bathers). Consequently, the beach scenes were pushed back to the end of the entire shooting schedule, when the water would be bearable. That meant two things: the first seagoing sequences would be pushed up, as would the shark's first appearances. That was a serious change, since it called for the *Orca* to be ready two weeks early and for Bruce the Shark to be similarly prepared.

Joe Alves and the art gang had made casts of the *Orca* and were preparing a fiberglass duplicate. They had been told it couldn't be done, but since Joe had never built anything like it before, he went under the assumption it could be done. And it was. When it was finished, the *Orca II* was a perfect replica, above the waterline, of *Orca I.* When it was time for it to work in front of the cameras, *Orca II* obediently sank and was recovered for another take twenty-four times, behaving gallantly under fire, tension, and shark attack. It was so realistic that Ward Welton, who had painted both boats, had jumped aboard *Orca II* and tried to start it and make it work, thinking it was *Orca I,* which was a real boat. Now that's realism.

Poor Murray Hamilton was most anxious about the progress of the film. His original commitment had been based on the outmoded production board, and as his original few weeks stretched into a month or more, he faced enormous conflicts with other, satisfying parts on the legitimate stage.

Playing the mayor of Amity, he had gotten trapped on the island and would unwind in the evenings as best he could. One night, after a particularly intense unwinding session, he was making his way back to his hotel when he happened to spot a cute little doggie rummaging around an unattended garbage can. Murray bent to pet the little doggie, which had this cute white stripe running down its back. Yup. It was a skunk, and Murray caught a full blast from the little furry creature. He was so unwound at the time that he didn't perceive his new fragrance, and he continued back to the hotel and climbed the unsteady stairs to his room, where he began to notice an awful stink. Opening the window didn't help, nor did changing his clothes. So he went downstairs wrapped in a blanket and slept on the couch in the lobby, until the arriving morning-shift desk clerk woke him, pointing out that the lobby was probably a poor place for a gentleman who had been unwinding to greet the dawn and the hotel patrons, if one were dressed only in a blanket and the unmistakable aroma of skunk. A few dozen showers later and with a good suit sorrowfully burned, along with the blanket, Murray was ready to face his day off.

There were uncomfortable pressures on all of us, but Murray probably suffered the worst indignity. For a gentle and talented actor like himself to be a stinker, even for a few hours, must have been a humiliation. Bad enough the character of Larry Vaughn, the mayor, was a stinker. I don't believe Murray will ever bend over to pet a strange little doggie again. As I recall, he was a happy man the day he left the island. (He would return weeks later for a few extra shots during the Fourth of July Beach Scene, but he knew that would be short, and he was right.)

Richard Dreyfuss began coming to dinner less often; as the Vineyard season opened, the island started filling up with summer people, bars and restaurants threw open their winter shutters, waitresses arrived from the mainland, and lots of them had seen *American Graffiti*, which was good news for young Rick. No longer dependent on our company, or on long drinking bouts with Robert Shaw full of mutual actor-insults and theater trivia, Ricky was free to cruise, which he did with a vengeance. The Vineyard's kind of hang-loose—he was a resident movie star, and nobody could say that he was inaccessible. So he made out all right. The crew was making out all right, too; most of them were in their late thirties and early forties, unmarried, earning good money, and far from home. Even the married guys were mostly unmarried while on location. The Teamsters, most of them from the Boston area, had their own recreation, with companions quietly shipped in from the mainland. There have been a couple of marriages resulting from the *Jaws* company's visit to the Vineyard, with a couple of Kelly House waitresses and a Colonial Inn barmaid traveling to Hollywood with their new husbands. (In the first few months, the generator man and his barmaid friend would serve as a dual clearing-house; he would tell her which crew members fancied which local girls, and she would confide in him which island girls liked which crew members. It was a happy arrangement.) After the initial flurry of friendship, most of the crew settled in with steady girlfriends. Up at the Log Cabin, we above-the-line types fell into bed alone at 9:30 P.M. and stared at each other's faces over hot tea and Adele's leftover desserts. It was grim.

One night, Robert Shaw, an accomplished novelist and playwright on his own, got into a serious discussion with an old-time Martha's Vineyard regular, the distinguished American playwright Thornton Wilder. Even though Thornton is in his eighties, he still likes his cup of cheer, and by the end of the evening poor Robert had difficulty walking (although he and Thornton understood each other perfectly. Their discussion consumed the better part of an evening and a bottle.) "I'm fine!" Robert would roar. "Just get me to the bloody pisser!" A local crew man was there to help, and when the evening was over, Robert's driver took him home. Thornton walked, I believe, but he had help—he uses a cane normally, and the extra support was all that he needed to navigate.

With the real tourist season nearly on us, the island's regular celebrities began turning up. Ruth Gordon and Garson Kanin, Lillian Hellman, Walter Cronkite, John Chancellor, Carly Simon and James Taylor, and visitors from Hollywood: producer/director Phil D'Antoni, directors Brian DePalma and Jim McBride, cameraman Vilmos Zsigmond, producers Michael and Julia Phillips . . . all friends from old projects, come to watch the fun and discuss new projects. Sundays became a day for athletics, with the *Jaws* softball team taking on all locals: Edgartown Bartenders and Bouncers, Oak Bluffs Layabouts, Tisbury Carpenters, Menemsha Sailors, whatever. The names were as informal as the teams. One game ended after the first inning stretched several hours, with the score around 45 to 30 (not much pitching, some days).

Sometimes local heavies would come to dinner at our house, sometimes we'd go have dinner or drinks with them. An argumentative James Reston, at about hour three of a four-hour cocktail party, took Dick Zanuck to task for not seeing to it that the movie industry celebrated the bicentennial of the republic. In vain did Dick try to explain that there is no "movie industry" with any kind of monolithic cohesiveness. Hollywood is all sharks and no marks, a lot of individually-centered studios and producers and stars each trying to do what's best for them. To expect this bizarre stronghold of free-enterprise endeavor to put aside its differences and work together on a freebie project like the Bicentennial was unthinkable, Zanuck said. "Nonsense," Reston replied. "Surely you could do something." "No," said Dick. "Yes," said Reston, and so it went until we excused ourselves and left. Outside, in the cool fresh air of the street, Dick stopped for a moment as we said good-byes. "He really doesn't understand a thing about movies," he said, and we all went home.

One night the police chief of Edgartown, a kindly old-timer, recently appointed, came for dinner, and we discussed all kinds of Vineyard trivia. The subject of the incident at Chappaquiddick Bridge came up, and a jovial, mild, easy-going local turned into an angry man before our eyes. He had not been on the force in Edgartown when that car went off the bridge; he was working on one of the other village forces. But he recalled some details that none of us recalled reading in the national press, and he was most upset about what had happened to the official records. According to the chief, every scrap of paper connected with Ted Kennedy, the bridge, Mary Jo, and the rest of it has been cleanly lifted from the files.[37] If you were to research that night that changed a presidential candidacy solely on the Edgartown police records, the jurisdiction where it occurred, you'd find nothing but a blotter entry on a radio log reporting a vehicle accident at Chappaquiddick Bridge, said the chief. No names, no police reports, no diver's reports, no statements by parties concerned, nothing. Only a three- or four-word notation on a record where a missing page would be too conspicuous. It was this tampering with the records that made the chief angrier than I've ever seen him. Of course, everybody on the island has his own inside information on that night, and the other best-seller on the Vineyard all summer was a book always displayed next to *Jaws* in every store, a cheap exposé titled *Teddy Bare*. If we hadn't come along, Chappaquiddick would still be the biggest event on the island since the hurricane of 1938 destroyed Menemsha.

We tried to show movies at the house to break the monotony. We had a 16-mm projector belonging to one of the cameramen, and we asked Universal to send some 16-mm prints from their library. We kept asking, until weeks later, they finally sent us a copy of *Spartacus* and a print of *Ma and Pa Kettle down on the Farm*. Steven asked Alan Ladd, Jr., over at Twentieth Century Fox, and all of a sudden there were fifteen or twenty features like *Patton* and *The French Connection*. I guess it all depends on who you know. Fox wanted Steven to do a film there, and I suppose this was their way of expressing affection for his talents.

We were running out of things to shoot on land, June was rolling to a conclusion, and the original schedule was out the window. Months earlier, the week before we left Hollywood, Steven had looked at the shooting schedule and predicted in a meeting with Sid Sheinberg that he'd be four or five days behind by the time we went to sea to shoot the third act. Sure enough, that's roughly where we were. Four or five days is $200,000, but that's not an unusual overage on a $3.5 million picture. But we weren't through yet. The shark had yet to undergo a thorough seaworthiness test, the *Orca I* was still wet with paint, and we had just about run out of things to shoot on land. There was only the Fourth of July Beach Scene left. The *Orca I* was hurriedly completed and the crew began working, doing interiors and deck stuff, as Steven began shooting everything he could without the shark. This included the now-famous scene in which Quint gives a long monologue about being aboard the USS *Indianapolis* when it was torpedoed at the end of World War II.[38] Robert Shaw was beside himself. His visa was running out, and Irish resident or no, one morning soon he would wake up owing the U.S. Government and the I.R.S. taxes on the money he had earned both on *The Sting* and *The Taking of Pelham One Two Three*. Every day that he wasn't required on the island, Robert would fly to Bermuda or Montreal, just to get out of the country for a few days and keep his worktime days in the U.S. down within the required limit. But it was to no avail. Despite his plaintive long-distance calls from all over the Western Hemisphere, "How's it going, Steven?" "Slowly, Robert," one day he woke up owing Uncle Sam an unhealthy bundle. But by this time, he was well into penalty payments from the *Jaws* company, and as the days stretched on to the horizon, the accountants in the Tower squirmed, Robert's agent smiled, Dick and David frowned, and the I.R.S. chuckled in evil glee. About this time, Peter Benchley arrived on the island.

Film Stills

for the 25th Anniversary Edition

The slate—also called "sticks" or a "clap board"—with a whimsical *Jaws* touch replacing normally simple black-and-white stripes.

Robert Shaw as Quint, the commercial fisherman with shark issues.

Carl Gottlieb as Meadows, editor and publisher of the Amity newspaper.

Richard Zanuck, producer, surrounded by a display of merchandising materials—cups, towels, books, and poster art—in the era before action figures, lunch boxes, and screen savers.

Craig Kingsbury as Ben Gardner, whose severed head and neck caused as many screams as any movie icon in history. Craig's not an actor but a crusty old salt we found on Martha's Vineyard who had a way with words, many of which found their way into Quint's dialogue.

Richard Dreyfuss as Hooper, the scrappy young oceanographer, here pretending he knows something about seamanship and instrumentation.

Bruce the shark and Robert Shaw, both relaxing between takes on the ruined afterdeck of the *Orca*.

Bruce and director Steven Spielberg enjoy a private moment, as crew and cast aboard the *Orca* stand by and Joe Alves checks Bruce's makeup. Is Bruce taking direction? Don't you believe it.

The S.S. *Garage Sale*, work boats, and the shark platform, all at sea with the full crew, trying to make something happen. Special effects master Bob Mattey is in the center, left of the tank, wearing a hat and holding up a line. Maybe that will help.

Richard Zanuck, the writer (with an ice cream bar), Lorraine Gary, and Sid Sheinberg (with a cigar) on location, waiting for something to happen. This is how most time is spent on any movie set in the history of taking pictures with a shooting schedule of more than twenty-five days.

Richard Zanuck, Murray Hamilton, Roy Scheider, the writer, Richard Dreyfuss, and Steven Spielberg on location. The actors are in costume and out of character; the producer is not in costume but deeply in character, studying something on the set and wondering if it will affect the budget.

A photo that is such a cliché it had to be included here. Found in every book about filmmaking, the generic title for this shot is The Director at the Camera, Studying a Shot. Here Steven Spielberg is the one looking through the lens while cinematographer Bill Butler waits his turn in the background.

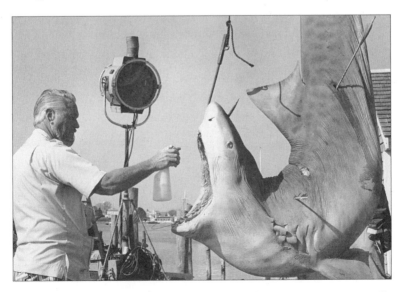

Makeup artist Del Armstrong freshening up the rotten appearance of a three-day-old dead shark hanging on the town dock.

Making a shot aboard the *Orca*, camera barge and gear in the foreground. Every light and line is moved for every new set-up or change of camera position; on land, on sea, or in the air, movies are still made by hand.

Bill Butler pointing arcs and reflectors. The cameraman's ultimate responsibility—painting with light.

In effect, a transport coffin for a fresh, dead shark. A charter flight stands by to put the fish in the movies.

Either some divers with minutes to live, oblivious of the great white shark behind them, or some grips setting up for a shot with Bruce in the MGM tank.

Sink the *Orca*, raise it up, and sink it again. Bruce resting mid-lunge on the afterdeck while the crew films the death of Quint.

Richard Dreyfuss as Hooper and Gottlieb as Meadows, preparing to film a scene that never made it into the film, aboard the *Fascinatin' Rhythm*. The camera boat is in the background.

Hooper pretends to steer *Fascinatin' Rhythm* alongside the wreck of Ben Gardner's boat. Gottlieb reaches for a grip, and an anxious Brody sits in the stern. Marine technical advisor Freddy Zendar crouches out of view, actually piloting the boat.

Oops! The actor/writer miscalculates the wind, drift, and distance. His center of gravity temporarily misplaced, Gottlieb goes headfirst over the side and into the water while the camera records the moment.

Roy Scheider and Fred Zendar lend Gottlieb a hand while Richard Dreyfuss is at the helm, trying to hold her steady as she goes.

If you wanted to be dramatic, you could say a life hangs in the balance as Gottlieb is pulled out of the water. Or you could note that he's found a foothold and is climbing aboard.

Saved! The sequence was later rewritten to eliminate Gottlieb, reshot as a night scene, and the film was better for it.

Joe Alves, Richard Zanuck, and Steven Spielberg in front of the S.S. *Garage Sale*, probably mulling a production design issue.

Actor, author, writer: Roy Scheider, Peter Benchley, and Carl Gottlieb on South Beach, discussing the script. Peter's holding his pages with obvious respect.

David Brown and Richard Zanuck waiting patiently on the set between takes, which was more often than not.

Steven Spielberg, Roy Scheider, Richard Zanuck, Valerie and Ron Taylor on the beach.

William Gilmore, Steven Spielberg, and Verna Fields studying a film clip on the beach, probably to match a previously shot sequence.

Steven Spielberg, Richard Dreyfuss, and Roy Scheider discussing the action. You know it's a serious actors' moment because Dreyfuss is smoking.

The auteur and the author: Steven Spielberg and Peter Benchley on the beach set, Steve pointing.

Bruce with a mouthful—Steven lounges in the water with a friend.

Everything works! Bruce in action, swimming past the *Orca*; Robert Shaw on the bow with a harpoon gun; the camera in the foreground, getting the shot.

Richard Dreyfuss, Murray Hamilton, Roy Scheider, and Steven Spielberg, looking off-camera at the defaced billboard.

Richard Zanuck and David Brown finally seated in correct billing order, with the heroic tug *Whitefoot* between them in the background.

"Excuse me, you're in the shot...." Although the *Orca* was supposed to be alone at sea, occasional day sailors might ruin the illusion (but at the same time create a scenic nautical photo opportunity).

CHAPTER TWELVE

"You're Peter Benchley, Aren't You? What Do You Think of All This?"

(June 21–28, 1974)

Amongst the scenes in the novel that survived the rewrites was a sequence on the Fourth of July beach, in which a local television news team brings a mobile unit down to film the controversy at Amity over the killer shark. Both Vaughn, the mayor, and Hooper the oceanographer give their sides of the story, Vaughn proclaiming the shark dead and the beaches open, Hooper insisting that they're not safe. In the final draft and in the film, Vaughn makes his statement, and Hooper is out patrolling a line of spotter boats with shark repellent, trying to do anything he can to prevent another attack, while Brody coordinates the effort on land.[39] To play the part of the TV newscaster, it was decided to try Peter Benchley. It was his original story, and it would be nice if he could be in it. There would be a little added press for the picture based on his participation as an actor, and, to top it all off, he was perfect for the part. A former features reporter for the *Newsweek* syndicated TV service, he was an experienced interviewer and his appearance is just right: tall, athletic, Eastern born-and-bred, just the right blend of bookish Harvard intellectual and tennis-playing, scuba-diving athlete. Next to Peter Benchley, Robert Redford looks like some swarthy Mediterranean type. So Peter said he'd be happy to do the part. He had been out plugging the book, since it was still on the best-seller list, and doing an ABC Sports special on diving and sharks. I'm sure he felt it would be nice to get paid SAG scale for coming up and seeing what we had done to his novel, and having had a taste of the media cookie as an author/personality on the talk-show circuit, the idea of being on the wide screen in color and Panavision probably was a tasty bit of frosting.

Naturally enough, there was some anxiety about his arrival. Peter was the author of all of this, and everything—sharks, budgets, schedules, problems—grew out of a desire of some way-above-the-line executives to bring his story to the screen. The process of transition was not entirely unexpected, nor was Peter a total stranger to the Hollywood development of a literary property. His father, remember, had written the novel that was made into *The Russians Are Coming*, so he was probably well cautioned as to what he might expect the moment he sold the rights to *Jaws* to Zanuck/Brown.

But intellectually understanding something is different from seeing it actually going down. It's one thing to sit alone and type "the beach in front of Scotch and Old Mill Roads was speckled with people"; it's another to stand on a beach pretending it's summer, with a band playing and a dozen cabanas and hundreds of yards of boardwalk and concession stands and bathhouses and a parking lot with trashbaskets, all built, painted, trucked in and put up, with every person on the sand being paid to be there, to watch a helicopter fly by and know that it too was specially summoned, as well as the million dollars' worth of trucks and equipment and generators hidden behind the dunes, and a fleet of coast guard boats with crews patrolling, all there to make it look like the beach is speckled with people. It's bloody well impressive. It may not be exactly what you had in mind when you wrote the novel, or even when you read it later, but there it all was.

Steven had added a full-scale panic and a complicated bit
of business involving the beach freaking out while the shark
coasts almost unseen into an adjacent estuary. It's a complicated plot development that's too long to summarize here,
but there it was, and Peter was in it. He was to be speaking
dialogue I had written for him, in a scene that didn't occur
that way in his book, so who knew how he'd react. It was my
first meeting with him; Steven had worked with him and assured me he was a swell guy, and, indeed, he was. Later. At
first, he was a trifle testy.

The reason he was miffed is simple, and not our fault. He
knew we were changing everything around. In the April 21
New York Times Magazine piece he had commented ruefully
that "A finer hand than mine is at work on it now, someone
who is doing what they call a dialogue polish, which is like
referring to gang rape as heavy necking." The "finer hand"
business is a little *noblesse oblige,* but as the principal "rapist"
of the previous drafts of the screenplay, I could appreciate
his concern. Having grown up in the harsh realities of television, I understood rewriting; however much you say it does-
n't matter, it always does, and each time you clench a little
inside. And rare indeed is the writer who will sit back with
his friends over Irish coffee and remark casually, "Oh, yes, I
saw it—did a terrific job changing everything, didn't they?
Marvelous. I must thank them." But if you can't stand being
rewritten, you can only write novels or poetry, or produce
and direct your own pictures, which is not the beginner's
way.

No, the reason Peter was put off was outside of what we
were doing on the island. *Newsweek* magazine had come to
the Vineyard to interview Steven and do a piece on the picture, which appeared the week Peter arrived. Besides revealing the name of prestigious writer number two (Howard
Sackler), the article quoted Steven incorrectly and printed a
lot of misinformation. In the second paragraph, *Newsweek* reports Steven saying, "Peter Benchley's view of his book was

not my view of the movie I wanted to make from his book . . . (he) didn't like any of his characters, so none of them were very likeable. He put them in a situation where you were rooting for the shark to eat the people—in alphabetical order!"

None of this sits well with Peter, understandably enough, so before he gets a chance to meet any of us or say hello, a reporter from the *Los Angeles Times* catches up with him, at lunch on the beach. Now it's Peter's chance to get in a few licks, so he takes Steven to task. "Spielberg needs to work on character," it is reported in the Calendar section of the L.A. *Times* the following week. "He knows, flatly, zero . . . He is a twenty-six-year-old who grew up with movies. He has no knowledge of reality but movies . . . Wait and see, Spielberg will one day be known as the greatest second-unit director in America." Now these are harsh words indeed, doubly harsh when it's considered that they will appear in Hollywood's own hometown paper, in the entertainment magazine section, on the cover, which the folks in the industry turn to first every Sunday over bagels and coffee. And remember, at this point Steven and Peter have not been in the same room since they worked on the first draft of the screenplay four months ago.

The *Los Angeles Times* reporter splits, and now it's dinner-time at the Log Cabin, and Peter and Zanuck and Brown are all invited for a formal "Hi there, how's it going." Try to get the picture: Here is Peter, tired, hot, fresh off a plane (he hates flying), a little piqued over Steven's *Newsweek* piece, and feeling only a little better 'cause he's just zinged Steven pretty good in the industry hometown paper. He walks into the Vineyard's coziest log cabin, where we give him a drink and Rick Dreyfuss invites him to play poker. (As much as Peter hates flying, he loves poker.) There's my typewriter in the corner, with all sorts of lunatic cartoons and slogans and reminders Scotch-taped to the log walls. (I like to wallpaper my work area with my work, or distraction from it. It's better than staring into space.) Obviously, it's a fellow writer's little padded cell, and here's the fellow writer, also playing poker, and being a nice guy. And here comes Adele, with some delicious melted cheese on toast rounds and more drinks, and now it's Dick and David in the door with warm hellos, and pretty soon we're all aglow with good feeling and old Scotch and funny poker table talk and Adele's melted Gruyère Exquisiteness. What's not to like?

And here comes Steven and Verna, fresh from the editing room, where they've been looking at some good dailies. They're smiling, and Steven's tired and vulnerable, and he's been busting his buns in the hot sun to get this picture made, and we're over-schedule, and it's the end of the day, and out on the lawn the sun is setting in a rosy haze over the nature preserve, and Nantucket Sound is quietly lapping the shore. Steven's first words are a clarification of what he really said, all the stuff *Newsweek* left out, and from there on everything thaws and we're all one happy family again. The next day Peter calls the *Los Angeles Times* guy to explain that he's not so angry as all that, and that some of what he said might've been a little offhand, and the *Los Angeles Times* guy dutifully writes it all down, and at the tail end of the story that appears the following week, all the insults stay in, with a lame little disclaimer, and a final snide editorial aside that intimates that since novelist and director are in the same raft, they've agreed not to rock the boat. But no matter. *Los Angeles Times* or not, we are all good friends, and in the days to come, we play a lot of poker and spend a lot of good times together, waiting on the beach to do the scene. The few days Peter's supposed to be there stretch into a week, as bad weather rolls in and we can't shoot a sunny Fourth of July beach scene in gray sky and driving rain, and there's nothing else left to shoot except the shark, and he's almost ready. Finally, Peter's part in the scene is finished, and it's off to friends and family and plugging the book, for all our collective good. For what it's worth, we're all still friends.

Months later, in the final stages of postproduction with the picture almost ready to come out, a filmmaker magazine called *Millimeter* prints a long interview with *Jaws* director Steven Spielberg, during the course of which it quotes Steven as saying, "If we don't make this movie better than the book, we're in real trouble." Oh, damn. Here we go again, and with a year-old interview surfacing to agitate the pleasant relationship we've all enjoyed since the Vineyard. It's doubly annoying to Steven because the first sneak previews, in Dallas, are fantastic, with wildly enthusiastic audiences and rave preview cards. So Steven writes a letter to Peter. He apologizes for the tone of the interview, and includes a Jacques Cousteau reference; a snotty comment the great old diver had made in the media, putting down the book as a fantasy and Peter as inaccurate on the subject of sharks, which is patently untrue, since Peter knows a great deal about sharks and the fish stuff was almost universally acclaimed as real, gripping, exciting, and like that. Peter immediately responded, and I reproduce his letter to Steven here with his kind permission.

Thanks for your letter, I don't see *Millimeter* (in fact, your mention of it was the first I'd ever heard), so whatever vicious, putrid, scabrous, scurrilous, subversive slime you ladled on me would probably have escaped my view. Nevertheless, forewarned is . . . etc. You were thoughtful to write.

In fairness, though, you should know that I have employed mercenaries to prepare a broadside about you, revealing, at last, the sordid truth about your personal life. It'll all be there—whips, leather sneakers, shorty-nighties and crunchy peanut butter. I'm aiming for the June issue of *Jack & Jill*.

I have yet to see the picture, but I'm scheduled to go to a distributors' screening next Wednesday. From all

I've heard, you have fashioned a masterpiece, for which I am (obviously) glad and grateful.

The Cousteau business is perplexing and annoying. Unspecific as his remarks have been, they're still reckless and inaccurate. I've written him a letter, asking him to cite specifics, but he hasn't replied. It's curious, for never in the past has he claimed or manifested any expertise about Great White Sharks. Meanwhile, I'm marshalling expert testaments about the accuracy of the book, not that I seriously expect a chance to use them.

Anyway, it will soon—God willing—be water under the proverbial bridge. Again, thanks for writing.

Best,
Peter Benchley

As of this writing, Peter and Jacques have not yet had it out, but I expect it to be spear guns at twenty fathoms, with a great white shark standing by to carry off the survivor.[40]

CHAPTER THIRTEEN

"The Doomsday Plan, and Why."

(June 29–July 31, 1974)

Years ago, one of Broadway's great play doctors and original writers commented that the classical three-act structure of a well-made play could be summed up this way: In Act One, you get a guy up in a tree. In Act Two, you throw rocks at him. In Act Three, you get him down again.[41] When I told this to Steven, he observed that making *Jaws* was a four-act structure. "In Act One, I get into a tree, and for the next three acts, people throw rocks at me." I think he was identifying a little closely with the picture, but at the time, we were sitting in front of an editing machine trying to figure out how to solve certain problems that needed to be fixed before the movie was finished, and it was more than a year since he had started work full-time on the movie. He was more than a little tired. But, in looking back over that final act of the movie, the seagoing sequence that took two and a half months to shoot and doubled the budget, he was right in recalling the pain, the frustration, the physical hardship, and the dogged weariness that went into making those last few reels work. What had come before was as nothing when you look at the problems of *Orca I*, *Orca II*, Bruce, Rick, Roy, and Robert, the wind, tides, and weather.

That phase of the picture began when the last beach stuff was wrapped. After that, there was no place to go except to the shark. He had to eat the man in the estuary, so we could all go down to the sea in ships, and shoot the last forty-seven pages of the script.

As we were finishing the last beach scenes and shooting a few scenes on the *Orca* without the shark or special effects, the gang under Bob Mattey at Shark City had put the finishing touches on the shark. (I'll refer to it in the singular, although there were three versions, described earlier. Only one worked at any time, so on any given shooting day, there was one shark.) Dick and David were demanding to see tests, which meant that the shark would have to be put in the water and operated for a second-unit camera, so we could have some idea of what it looked like on film. The special effects department was incurably optimistic, promising an early test, swearing everything would be "go" whenever necessary. But, as Joe Alves recalled months later, "You ask Bob Mattey what time it is, and he'll tell you how to build a watch." Affectionately, Joe was recalling those times when a simple question about the shark's behavior would draw a lengthy response about hose diameter, flotation, fluid mechanics, and mechanical resistance. All anybody wanted to know was when could we see the damn thing working in the water.

Soon enough, a couple of barges would be laboriously towed to sea, a few miles off Oak Bluffs, where work was in progress. The sea sled was tested, then the underwater platform was towed out. Remember that this was 12 tons of welded steel platform, flotation tanks, a wide track, a rolling dolly arm with a pivot, and the connecting control cables and hoses with their attendant hardware and fittings. It would be towed to an appropriate spot in the ocean where the depth and the horizon sightlines were right, lined up so that the sharks would travel the right way, then sunk in position like a caisson or bridge underpinning. Then the shark, in its seagoing cradle, would be positioned over the sunken, leveled platform and fastened onto the dolly arm. Then the camera boats and the *Orca* could move into position and set up for a shot.

It was not an easy operation, even after months of practice, and the first time it was an extraordinary experience. Dick Zanuck had been on the radio from the mainland, hanging around the production office, calling out a constant "Are you ready for us to come out yet?" The special effects department, whose prestige and skill were on the line, would respond, "Having a few technical problems. Soon." The training period for the special effects operators was that May 15 to June 15 period when we were shooting on land, except that the beast didn't get wet until June 15, two weeks away from its scheduled debut on film, in an actual shot on the schedule. Secrecy was still important, and the company's press representative, a genial pipe-smoking Al Ebner, who served as unit publicist, had to be evasive full-time, trying to steer visiting journalists away from Shark City. Those reporters who came up on a free junket paid for by Universal were generally content to hang out in the Kelly House, interview one of the stars, get drunk with Al, and go home. The more enterprising, investigative types were a little more hard-nosed. Guys from Boston and nearby local papers, out on assignment, would use island sources, dig around outside the official company line, locate Shark City and the boathouse where the sharks were being painted and finished, and try to steal a few pictures. On the day that Dick Zanuck finally chose to come out to Shark City for a personal inspection of the progress of the special effects department, he found a hundred tourists snapping away with their Instamatics while the shark, in full view, was laboriously being loaded onto its seagoing cradle. That was the day the *Christian Science Monitor* got its bootleg photos of the shark, and Dick was very mad. There were memos issued, reprimands all around, and an immediate order to shroud the

shark whenever it was moved. That night, Joe Alves got seriously, rigidly plastered, and cried.

The shark *had* to work. There was no question about it.
Several millions of dollars had been spent on that assumption, and there was a two-thirds-completed movie waiting on
that supposition. The pressure was on Bob Mattey to deliver,
and July 1, they decided to float the submersible platform
out to its correct location, in Cow Bay, with the island at its
back, and a 180 degrees of unbroken horizon looking out to
Nantucket Sound and the Atlantic Ocean. Out it went, and
slowly they began to fill the flotation tanks, blowing the air
out, letting the water in, dropping the twelve-ton, 30' x 60'
steel mass onto the ocean floor. One side started to sink
faster than the other. The whole platform took on a dangerous list. Divers and riggers in wet suits started to scramble,
and a swift hand on the pneumatic controls deftly swung a
lever the wrong way. Instead of evening the rate of fill on the
tanks, it blew the last ballast out of the wrong side of the
platform, and all twelve tons of steel tipped over on its side
and slid into the icy-green ocean. As they watched it sink,
the radio crackled into life. "Hi—this is Dick Zanuck and
David Brown. Is it all right to come out now? We've got a
boat standing by . . ."

With the gods of the sea smiling, the platform was righted
and a damage survey revealed nothing serious. It was set
into place, leveled off, anchored, and the shark and the *Orca*
brought out. Along came a special effects barge with all the
auxiliary control equipment and a camera barge, as well as
some support boats, among them the majestic ocean-going
tug *Whitefoot*. The skipper of the *Whitefoot* was a righteous salt
we called Cap'n Roy. He was our cook Adele's brother-
in-law, and her first comment when she heard he was coming on the picture was, "You'll have your hands full with
him. He's a hard-headed son-of-a-gun." And indeed he was.
We had not started the shooting with the *Whitefoot*, relying
instead on some local fishing boats and auxiliary craft that

the unit manager had booked. The tug *Whitefoot* was too expensive for charter anyway, it seemed then. Built in 1961 especially for deep-sea salvage work, she had massive twin screw diesels and a mobile crane capable of lifting eight or ten tons dry weight. She was a no-kidding-around working vessel, the pride of the syndicate that owned her and the apple of Cap'n Roy's eye. When she wasn't making movies, she was on long cruises with the Woods Hole Oceanographic Institute or on secret business with the U.S. Navy. After the first weeks at sea filming a few small scenes (like the one in which I got dunked), it became obvious that the first boats hired were not tough enough to do the job, and Bill Gilmore, with characteristic authority (remember, he had dispatched a private jet from Boston to Sarasota, Florida, to bring back a dead shark),[42] got us the *Whitefoot*. She was so big and sturdy she could actually give us a quiet lee and some still water to work in, if it came to a pinch. She was a stable camera platform, and her crane could pick up an 8,000-pound generator with ease and swing it anywhere we wanted to put it.

Cap'n Roy had a neat little stateroom with a private bunk and dainty curtains and brightly polished brasswork and varnished and polished wood; it was his home, that boat, and he didn't want any greasy grips stomping through it leaving cigarette ashes and fingerprints and empty coffee cups. The stars and director could retire to the Captain's Quarters, but the rest of the crew could just damn well be careful where they walked. Cap'n Roy insisted that electrical cable be neatly coiled when not actually in use, and kept shouting down from the bridge, "Mind the varnish, boys, mind the varnish!" His seamanship was, of course, spectacular, and the benefits of his experiences with the big tug outweighed the nuisance of his constant housewife's shrilling over his clean decks and his gleaming toilets. (The head on the *Whitefoot* was actually put off-limits to the crew, just like Officer's Country on a navy ship of the line, until a compromise was worked out. An extra deckhand was put on to keep the heavily used head shipshape, to pick up the Styrofoam cups, and maintain the purity of the varnish throughout.)

Finally, the shark was in the water. "Can we get a shot now?" asks Steven. "Not yet, got some technical problems," comes the reply, quick as a flash. And that was the only thing quick about the operation from then on. Consider the mechanics involved: First, is it going to be a good enough day to shoot? The weather reports must be checked to make sure there's going to be at least a modicum of light, no sudden storms, no catastrophic tides or winds. Of course, on Martha's Vineyard they're used to weird weather. Sometimes even the ferryboats can't run, during heavy winter storms or fogs, and for almost 400 years the hardy Yankees of the island have won a name as superb seamen and whalers, due to their early training in the same waters on which we were trying to shoot. But there we were, trying to get the movie shot, because it was, all things considered, one of the best places to do that, given our logistical problems.

Our first task each day, then, was to find out if the weather prediction was favorable. The company used every source available: marine forecasts, national weather service, local meteorologists, soothsayers, whatever worked. Gilmore was considering the entrails of a sheep, but was talked out of it. Barbara Bass, the second assistant director, claims to this day that a little Cape Cod AM Top-40 rock station that woke her up on her clock radio was the most accurate of all, but she was only second assistant director, so what she said didn't carry a lot of weight. Besides, who's going to risk a $50,000 shooting day on some Boss Jock with Platters That Matter?

Now, assuming the weather report's encouraging, the following operations have to happen concurrently: Teamsters have to collect the crew and drive them to small boats that will take them out to where the shark platform is sunk on the bottom of the sea, and to where the special effects barge is anchored nearby. This ferry service is limited by the number of people a Boston Whaler can hold safely. At the same time, the shark that's supposed to work is loaded onto the slings on its sea-going drydock, and a powerful fishing boat begins towing it out to the same location. Simultaneously, the director and actors are given their wake-ups and bundled into cars for their drive down to the dock, and their speedboat out to the location. Over at the boatyard, the *Orca I* is cranked over and started up and piloted out to the location, thirty-five minutes to open sea through an exhausting, annoying chop.

When everybody arrives at "The Location" (a nameless spot in the ocean marked by buoys and the anchored special effects barge), the decision has to be made (by the director, who's an artist and an engineer, not a seaman) as to where to put it all. The shark's movements are a constant: back and forth on the track running four fathoms down. Everything else must be planned around that—the position of the *Orca*, the camera, the angles, all this in relation to the horizon and the passage of the sun, so that a scene begun in light won't be in shadow by afternoon. Take into account, also, the problem of the sky—the action on film is supposed to cover a period of about thirty-six hours (one day, one night, and part of the next day), so it wouldn't do to have the sky in the background of the shot changing color and consistency, with clouds popping in and out, depending on who's talking.

Further: each static boat and barge must be anchored so as not to drift during the day (and there are two tides a day, with currents of five or six knots tugging one way and then the other). To "nail a boat down" requires four or more anchors, from the four quarters of the boat, stretched taut with some simultaneity. The *Orca*, which is supposed to be under way or adrift, can't have any visible anchors, so she has to be anchored below the waterline, which means divers in scuba gear tying anchors off to eyebolts set low on the hull, below the surface. Every anchor has to be set, not dropped, which means maneuvering in small boats with anchor and line to a spot that looks right, and dropping the anchor out of the small boat, hoping that when the tides and current start pulling, all four or five anchors will balance the tension between them and hold the boat or barge steady, without changing its orientation to the other boats and barges. This was repeated every shooting day. More than basic seamanship, you can be sure.

Grips and gaffers, crewmen who had never been to sea, became old salts quickly, and everybody wore wet suits or bathing suits most of the time. When this was all done, the shark could be loaded onto the dolly arm, and thirty control hoses coupled to it, making sure to keep water out of the lines, since the shark was powered by compressed air. (Electric motors would've shorted out in the constant salt water.) There was a complicated set of electronic sensing devices built into the underwater platform to give readouts showing position and speed, but thanks to a complicated ocean process called electrolysis and the steady diet of salt air and moisture, they had burned out weeks before; everything had to be operated by sight or instinct.

It was just this undeveloped instinct that put the shark into a dive early on and didn't pull him up in time. It was around noon; the whole morning had been spent ferrying everything into position and anchoring it down, and here comes the shark, with an enormous dimple in its chin, looking like an aquatic, toothy Kirk Douglas. Back into the shop for repairs. It's a $50,000 dent, counting the day's lost time. Film tests are coming in from the lab at the same time, and the shark's teeth are too white, they catch the light wrong in the water, and look too bright, too phony. Back to the shop. (Joe Alves has built a precision shark—real great whites have ten distinct types of teeth in their jaws; Joe has made at least seven different kinds, in two variations, one hard, for general use, one soft, for biting people.)

The July days begin to get longer and longer, with nothing to do. The special effects department continually underestimates the time required for a setup, so Steven and the cast and key crew (first assistant director, cameraman, camera operators) are constantly building up for a letdown, as the hours go by without a setup. At two grand or more per hour, it's no fun to just sit and watch the seagulls when you're worked up for a shot. Soon, Steven begins second-guessing the special effects guys. Bob Mattey says they'll be ready for a shot at 11 A.M., Steven tells the actors "after lunch," which makes them feel real good about getting up at 6:30 A.M. and shlepping out in an open boat. Robert Shaw's only distraction has been golf, a game he loves, and he and the assistant wardrobe man, Irwin Rose, are constantly out on the links together, even in the cold rain. ("Just like Ireland," Robert sighs wistfully, and has some hot tea or Scotch.)

Steven has been made into an enthusiastic trap- and skeet shooter, thanks to the preproduction urgings of fellow director and shooting enthusiast John Milius (who is in Spain at the same time as all this is going on, getting *his* thrills by directing an epic period adventure yarn with lots of shooting, riding, and Spaniards). John is on time and under budget, so he's OK; Steven is over and feeling the pressure, so he proposes to those of us who are interested that we set up a device to throw clay birds over the ocean from the stern of the *Orca*. He will bring out his Perrazi and his Browning shotguns, and there'll be a lunch-hour skeet shoot during our thirty-minute lunch break, just like on the luxury ocean liners, with pukka sahibs gunning from the stern. The crew hears this and quietly presents an ultimatum to the production manager: Steven brings loaded guns on board, they're not coming to work. In vain do we point out it's during lunch hour, it's safe, and all that. The crew is unmoved. They will grant him his phenomenal professionalism as a director; he is the youngest they've ever worked with. But when it comes to guns he's still a kid, the crew thinks, and no kids with guns on the cramped decks of the picture boat. So no shotgunning.

Bill Gilmore issues a No Beer edict at sea, and follows it up with a No Card Playing order, all in the interests of efficiency; the crew is hurt, and further deprived of idle recreation while anchors are set and special effects organized, so most of them take to either staring witlessly out to sea like marooned sailors or fishing over the side for sand sharks (little four-foot sharks that live in abundance in Nantucket Sound). Almost every shark caught is killed, and its guts used as bait to catch more sharks, which are also killed. It was the crew's revenge on an entire species. Fortunately, none of our divers got bit.

When the shark worked, it worked like this: fastened to the top of this mechanical arm, it could skim along the surface, diving and surfacing on command; the arm was attached to a trolley that ran on steel rails on the sunken platform, giving it a range of about seventy feet of movement in a straight line. The *Orca* would be positioned relative to the shark's path, and the camera placed where it could best record the action: in the water where it could see boat and shark, or on the boat where it could see men, boat, and shark in the water. The *Orca* would be anchored, or left free, in case a moving or passing shot was required. In the event that the boat would have to pass the shark, there would be a lot of clever seamanship involved, since a false move by the *Orca* could cause it to ram the shark mechanism, causing further delays. Frequently the boat would be towed to simulate free movement. In this case, the tow cable would have to be fastened below the water line or out of the shot, thereby creating more problems for riggers and special effects men. Naturally, all this work was accomplished by hand labor, men in wet suits, and divers. For all its mechanics, moviemaking is still a lot of manual labor.

The month drags slowly on. It's high season in Martha's Vineyard, so the company is paying premium prices for hotel rooms and meals, the bars are crowded at night, the streets are jammed, and the regular winter population of the island, about 6,000, has swelled ten times, to about 60,000. Every facility is crowded, every street is jammed with traffic, and every ferry from the mainland is bringing more people to stare at the work, get in the way, and make life tough on everyone. In addition, it's sailboat season, and the horizon is dotted with snowy canvas. It's not bad enough the America's Cup was held this year, attracting every yachtsman on the East Coast. They all stayed for the summer, it seems, and where we are shooting (between Oak Bluffs and East Chop) is the base leg of one of the most popular cruises in these waters, a Nantucket to Cape Cod run, or something like that. At first, the speediest boat in our squadron of motley rentals is dispatched to shoo them away, but you can't clear a thirty-mile horizon line, so what to do? The scenes being filmed require an empty horizon, the shark hunters must be alone at sea with their prey; the story demands it. One day, Steven decides that the endless parade of cutters, ketches, and yawls is too much. "Turn her around!" he orders. "Let's get it from another angle." So over the side go the divers to free the *Orca,* up come the anchors on the barges and support boats, out go the Boston Whalers to reset the flukes; for seven hours it's a mess of conflicting orders, splashing, motors roaring, and endless maneuvering, and as the last few anchors are being set, and the last barge nudged into position, Steven, sitting morose and alone on the bowsprit of the *Orca,* looks up in time to see the sun setting, losing the light, ending shooting for that day. Only there was no shooting—too many sails, too much time spent shifting boats.

So he learns his lesson, and every time they see a sail and the camera operator lifts his head from the eyepiece and says, "It's in," the cast and crew learn to sit down and wait until it's past and they can try again to get the shot. The rage and anxiety of the actors fighting the shark in the last act is honestly arrived at—it's not only a visualization of the characters' emotions in the script, it's the very real expression of the discontent with the process of filming. Later, Steven changes location to a windy, more perilous spot with heavier seas, but a less frequently used channel, with an uninterrupted view of the Atlantic horizon.

On shore, the frustrations are mounting with equal rapidity. There is a union requirement that any working production personnel be driven where he has to go—it's a reasonable Teamster contract demand ensuring the full employment of drivers. While on the payroll, no actor can take his own car and drive to location; a Teamster must take him, unless the actor is not on a work call and is officially released for the day. Joe Alves is the source of a grievance for driving his bicycle from the boat shed to the dock. "He's gotta have a driver. You're putting a man out of a job," comes the Teamster's lament. "What if he walks? You got jurisdiction over shoe leather?" replies the production man. "He can't go nowhere without a driver, that's all I know." Later it's resolved amicably, and the company enjoys good relations with its Teamsters, which is a good thing, because our Teamsters, with the exception of the studio men who drove the trucks out from the West coast, are all Boston men; enormous Boston Irish, with big hands, battered faces, and bodies that start small at the head and get very big down around the belly and bottom. Although they are tough cookies, they are also gentlemen on the job. Their off-duty hours were very much their own, with only a few dark hints about their private recreations and amusements.

Curiously enough, Richard Dreyfuss, the Beverly Hills kid who always wanted to be an actor, is the grandson of an old-time Teamster of some influence; his grandfather was a tough New Yorker who knocked heads with the best of them, and was an important figure in the organization of the West Coast Teamsters until he quit their board, so Ricky has some measure of respect. The rest of us are just polite, and we all have a comfortable working relationship for the rest of the picture.

More frustration. Every night after work, the shark is hauled out of the water and studied: paint peeled, minor scratches, looking bad, it's got to be dried out before anything can be done. The sharks are covered with the polyurethane and neoprene flesh, which manages to absorb some water. Heavy-duty oil-fired burners and blowers go to work as soon as the monster is hauled out of the water. The typical schedule for the special effects crew goes like this: 1 A.M. to 6 A.M.: shark washed, painted, spruced up. 6:30 A.M.: load onto cradle and begin towing to location. 8:00 A.M.: arrive at location and connect thirty control hoses. 9:00 A.M.: load shark onto dolly platform, operations test. Anytime after that until it's too dark to shoot: operate shark in connection with *Orca,* and whatever shots are scheduled for that day (i.e., "The Shark lunges past the bow, Quint fires another harpoon into its flank."). At the conclusion of the shooting day, disconnect the control hoses, hoist shark off the dolly arm onto the pontoon cradle, tow back to shore, secure everything for paint gang, start heaters going.

It was an around-the-clock operation, especially when the same shark worked two days running. They tried to work it out so the fish would rotate, but it didn't always come out right (nothing did in July), so problems came thick and fast. The dimple in the shark's chin was eventually pushed out like a dented fender, but it was never an easy job trying to repair the ravages of the ocean. Even Bob Mattey, who would never admit that anything was really wrong (Zanuck says, "He liked to give it to us a little at a time") said, later, that they had underestimated the power of the sea. Barnacles that would cut the divers' hands accumulated on the undersea platform. A special grease had to be applied to the dolly tracks while they were under water, by scuba-diving technicians. Growths of kelp and algae and seaweed would foul the works. The work barge with the controls on it was permanently anchored at sea and was christened the S.S. *Garage Sale,* officially, as it turns out, because there was a coast guard registry involved, so when someone said, "What'll we call this thing?" Someone else said "What does it look like?" And a third party said "A goddamn garage sale," and so it went on the records. The work barge had generators and compressors aboard, as well as spare welding tools and equipment, air pumps for recharging divers' tanks, heaters, and, eventually, a hot shower rigged for men who had been mucking around in the 55° water with grease and lubricants. The first time they tried towing the shark against the wind and tide, it simply burst, bending and twisting 1½" steel control rods. Tough stuff, the ocean.

Every night, with the last boat out from shore, a watchman would come to spend the night on the barge to prevent local marauders and predators from boosting expensive tools and equipment. As the picture ground on, things started to disappear with regularity: generators, folding boats, tools, nylon line, anything the local scroungers thought they could use. Tempers were wearing thin, and the company spent even more money replacing lost and stolen equipment. Finally, a tremendous summer storm blows in, with large swells and heavy running seas. The watchman stands it as long as he can, then makes it for shore. The barge is breaking up under him, the undersea platform is taking a terrible beating trying to hold its anchorage against the surge of storm and tide. In the morning, good old *Whitefoot* hitches its big diesels to the hulk, tows everything in, and we discover the flotation tanks are cracked and taking water. From then on, the work barge is pumped daily to keep it afloat.

And that's not all that's in trouble. All over, the picture shows signs of going down like the *Titanic*, but calm hands are at the helm, and cool heads are on the bridge. Steven is the Boy who Stood on the Burning Deck; Dick and David are like Nelson at Trafalgar, calm, resolute, never showing any outward signs of anguish or despair. The picture is clearly going to cost millions more than budgeted; how much is anyone's guess. But the strength of *Jaws* is greater than the *Titanic's*—we *are* unsinkable. The dailies (what there is of them) are looking good (and believe me when I assure you that the film being sent back from the Vineyard was studied very carefully by the executives in the Tower back at Universal). The book is a publishing phenomenon, holding steady in the Top Ten, twenty weeks on the charts and no signs of faltering. There is no delegation of executive troubleshooters come out to location to personally survey the problems. No anxious demands to see some cut sequences. Here we were, forty days over schedule and about a million and a half over on the budget, and it's *laissez-faire* time! It bespoke great confidence in the whole team and kept spirits up during the darkest days.

And the darkest days were dark indeed. In Bill Gilmore's office there was a map of the world, with every possible location from Indonesia and the Indian Ocean right up the American coast from the Caribbean to Nova Scotia. Every day Bill, Dick, and David would study it and try to figure out if they'd be better off to move the show to quieter waters, or a cheaper location, or someplace where the weather was better. The Doomsday Plan was formulated. It called for the company to shut down and go home, except for the special effects crew, who would just stay here and learn how to make the shark work right. Then in September, when the tourists and the sailboats and the high prices would be gone, everyone would reconvene on the Vineyard and we'd pick up where we left off, having worked on editing the rest of the picture in the meantime. The studio would ask SAG and the stars for some kind of waiver, and pick up their salaries again in the fall.

But it never came to that. Verna expressed her enthusiasm over the cut sequences that she was working on, and the studio trusted her. Steven maintained an ironclad resolve not to show incomplete footage to anyone until he felt it was ready and the sequence could stand on its own. Even Dick and David, the producers, wouldn't look at material unless Verna had Steven's OK to show it to them on her KEM. (The KEM is an editing table, a recent European addition to the tools of the trade, and is slowly replacing the Moviola as the editing standard. The table shows film on a little projection screen, like a TV set, and makes viewing your work a lot more comfortable.)[43] Dick and David, when they did see rough assemblages, saw promise and even fulfillment in the way the picture was coming together.

But all the while, the studio had it in its power to "pull the plug." That's a dread phrase in the industry, and it's an authority rarely delegated below studio head or vice-president in charge of worldwide production. It's an apt and simply descriptive phrase. It means Stop, Don't Do Any More, That's It. It means shutting off the money until the work so far has been assessed, and a decision is made as to whether or not to continue.

In rare cases, pictures have actually been scrubbed while in production. (Fox did it to a Marilyn Monroe vehicle called *Something's Got to Give*, and it cost $2 million to fire her and end it. But there was no way it could ever be finished, because later she committed suicide.) It's more customary to finish the picture any way possible, at the lowest possible cost, paste it together in some kind of order, and then try to get a few bucks back at the drive-ins. There's no way to release a picture that's incomplete, but a finished picture can be dumped on the airlines, as part of a television package, something. But nobody said the dread words, the dailies kept going back to the lab, the Tower kept looking at the dailies and the production reports, and every day we went down to the dock, ferried out to sea, and tried to get a shot or two before it got too dark.

As the days dragged by, normally quiet men began giggling and gabbing constantly. Guys like Vito (the talky wisecracking grip who would respond to any question with a question—"For a six-pack?") became strangely silent and spent long hours staring at the horizon or counting waves. Bill Tenney, the Gaffer, got hold of an electric bullhorn and instead of issuing simple directions to his men began broadcasting a running commentary on everything that was going on. Steven would invent shots, simple inserts that could be filmed without special effects, and although everyone thought they'd probably never be used in the film, folks went to work with a will, dressing the set, lighting it, adjusting the frame, placing the camera. It was something to do, and months later it turned out almost every shot was used, all of it fitting into Steven's calculated visual scenario.

CHAPTER FOURTEEN

"The Boatmen's Strike, the Sinking of the *Orca*, and the End of the Season."

(August 1974)

The camera crew was spectacular. The director of photography was a quiet gentleman who looked twenty years younger than he was, named William Butler. He and Steven had worked together in television, and Bill had just finished shooting *The Conversation* with Francis Ford Coppola. He refused to be rushed, took his time with every setup, and frequently produced footage that surprised and pleased the eye.

Operating the camera was a cameraman from the New York local. That very particular union requires East Coast members to do any work on the East Coast, regardless of the picture's origins. As a New York cameraman, he alternated between operating a camera and working as a director of photography. (Because of the scarcity of work for directors of photography in New York, the guys there have no status thing about operating once they've been promoted; they jump back and forth from director of photography to operator.) He was Michael Chapman, an Easterner with a pronounced Maine twang. He loved the Vineyard, went clamming in the few off-hours he had, and spent the entire picture, it seemed, balancing and hand-holding the Panavision camera (Panaflex).

Shots that would've been impossible with any conventional tripod or mount were made by the simple expedient of putting the camera on Mike's shoulders and letting the flexion of his legs and the control of his torso hold the dancing horizon steady in the frame. Try taking home movies on a small boat sometime, and you'll begin to appreciate the rock-steadiness of our own Michael, who operated the Panaflex in the water, on the boat, in the boat, under the boat, without ever succumbing to a jiggle or roll that would hurt the shot. Mike is the most widely-read and best-educated man I've met in movies, and a gentleman besides.

Jim Contner and Peter Salem, the assistant cameramen, knocked their brains out, and like the special effects crew, their day was never ended when we called "Wrap." The cameras would have to be cleaned and maintained and made perfect for the next day's shooting, and perfect is not a relative word. The camera has to function every time, for fear of missing an otherwise acceptable shot. An occasional jam or jiggle is tolerated, but never well; production time is too costly for that.

Each night, there would be telephonic press conferences between Steven and the production department. Bill Gilmore and Steven grew further and further apart as Bill pressed for an early end to the shooting and some salvation of the badly overstrained budget and Steven fought to make every hard-won shot count, remembering every detail of every frame, cross-filing them in his mind against the day when he would have to sit in an editing room with Verna in Los Angeles and try to make it work. Verna fretted at the dailies, since the carefully described sequence of shots outlined in the final shooting script bore little resemblance to the slates and scene numbers coming in.

Charlsie Bryant, the script supervisor, was responsible for keeping track of the entire enterprise in a carefully annotated copy of the script that is a bible and an encyclopedia of information for postproduction.[44] Because of space limitations on the *Orca* and the dangers of hopping back and forth from camera barge to *Orca* to shuttle ferry, Charlsie had to content herself with staying on the barge while Steve, Mike Chapman, and Bill Butler conferred on what the shot was to be; the slates began to bear little relationship to the scenes, and it was going to be Steven's responsibility and Verna's to cut it together some way, later. Then the boatmen went on strike.

The boatmen were a bunch of local youths, most of them in college, who had rented their fast Whalers or sportfishers to the company to ferry men and equipment back and forth. For themselves and their boats, they got a cool $90 per day, which ain't bad six days a week when you're on summer vacation. But they got to talking, and soon they heard what the Teamsters and the crew were getting (forgetting that Teamsters and movie crews don't work all that steady, and that movie crews spend a long time learning to do what they do). So they decided to strike for higher pay. Bill Gilmore, who knows how to say "No," told them that. They stopped working, and the overstressed production crew began the tiresome shuttle service, with only Barbara Bass's boyfriend, Jonathan, staying on (he was the actor in the opening scene, but he had a boat and knew how to run it, so he was hired to do that, too). After a few random threats of physical violence, the boat jockeys came back to work, but things were never the same. Petty sabotage increased, things kept disappearing, but although the strike leader threatened it, there was no appreciable increase in the number of sailboats on the horizon.

The production manager is like a straw boss or a first sergeant. Ostensibly up from the ranks as an A.D. or auditor, he belongs to the same union as the director but his function is to watch the budget and the schedule, restraining the overly creative director, goading the recalcitrant crew, and reporting to the producer, whose interest he serves. Bill Gilmore knows the ropes and can say "no" very convincingly.

Twice before he had solved production problems that way. The first time, he had to correct a blunder by the unit manager, who had negotiated a deal with the crew. The company would not pay for wet suits. So far so good. But it would rent wet suits from individual crew members if they had to wear them, paying them $50 per week for the use of their suits (which were undeniably necessary in the chilly waters). Well, Bingo! The crew ran out and all bought $85 wet suits, and by the second week they were in profits (unlike the movie). Bill Gilmore came on the scene, took one look, and called off the deal. Despite angry maneuvering by the shop stewards, a final price for wet suits was negotiated, and that was that for renting wet suits. A similar deal had been made for the rental of lead ballast for the *Orca*. Again, it had been rented for way over its purchase price, so Bill simply halted the rental and dared the owners of the lead to either sue him or go out and take their lead back. That worked out OK, too. There were times when Bill would tell Steven "No," and Steven would go to Dick and David, and they'd all work it out; it didn't make anyone any friendlier during the shooting. Steven recalls his happiest days as dim gray mornings when he'd get a call from the production office at 6:30 A.M. telling him there was no 7:00 A.M. pickup—he could sleep until 9:00; there were technical problems to iron out. On those days he would roll over in bed with a smile and try not to dream about the ocean.

Time out for a little history. Way back in the early days of movies, an assistant director had to send a day player home because he was too drunk to work. In that day's production report, the assistant director duly noted, "Actor X dismissed at 11 A.M., too drunk to work." The actor sued for slander and defamation of character (being drunk on the job is a serious offense, and in the Actors Equity Association it's the only reason for direct dismissal without further cause or remedy).

The actor won his suit and got some money out of the studio; since the assistant director was not a physician, he couldn't properly assess that elusive state known as "drunkenness," which even the highway patrol has difficulty in proving without elaborate measurements. The studio called in all its assistant directors and production people and issued a stern new policy: never make a direct adverse statement on a production report. Always say "apparently," or "appeared to be." Well, from that day on, production men have been brought up to say negative things with a qualifier in front of them, and that brings us back to our story.

Bill Gilmore is sitting in the office wondering where to finish the picture if the bad weather keeps up, when he hears the radio in the next room squawk into life. It's the first assistant director, Tom Joyner, out at sea filming with the first unit. "Bill Gilmore, Bill Gilmore," says the radio, and Bill can recognize a new note in Tom's voice. Like a married man who can smell trouble in a wife's "Good evening," Bill can tell that this is not some ordinary call about the schedule for tomorrow. "Joyner, this is Gilmore. What is it, Tom?" "Uh, Bill—the *Orca* is apparently sinking."

Apparently sinking? No sir. Going down like a ton of bricks. Not like the *Orca II*, which was built to sink, but like the *Titanic*, which was not. The shot-in-progress was one of the climatic moments in the picture: the *Orca* violently tipped to one side by crushing underwater blows from the angry shark. The resulting list throws the three men off their feet, risking their lives if they should fall into the ocean with the shark. The brute attack on the boat also indicates the blind fury of the fish, its fighting instincts driving it into an attack on its tormentor, the boat. Since Bruce is not seen in the shot, he's home being painted and getting his innards rewelded. The boat is rigged to tip by a complicated arrangement of underwater cables, and several cameras are cued to roll simultaneously, giving us plenty of coverage of the complex effect.

It takes a long time to set the shot, but finally it's ready. The big moment comes, everything is triggered, and whoops! There goes the *Orca!* Under the surge and strain of the gag, one of the eyebolts in the hull anchoring the boat pulls out, along with a big section of planking, leaving a table-sized hole in the hull below the waterline, which is not a good place to have a hole in your boat. In minutes it's obvious something's gone wrong. The boat is still listing badly, tipping drunkenly over to one side, and slipping further and further over. The superstructure is a trifle heavy, so the vessel is balanced badly, plus there's a lot of men and equipment standing on the flying bridge and there's not much ballast in the hold. Someone shouts, "She's going over!" and everyone starts to bail out. Jim Contner, Peter Salem, and Michael Chapman are trying to save the cameras with their priceless film inside. Rick and Robert jump into the ocean, and the rest of the crew is right behind them. Roy Scheider is trapped in the cabin, since that's where he's supposed to be for that part of the shot, only now he's *really* trapped in the cabin, but he manages to fight his way clear. In another minute, the boat capsizes and sinks, and the sea is full of swimming men, small boats maneuvering to effect rescues, and a lot of debris and parts of tripods, slates, scripts, coffee cups, lights, cameras, and action.

Two Arriflex cameras are down there in the briny deep, with the precious film inside, and a diver recovers them. One is the "A" Camera, which is the principal camera responsible for recording the crucial part of the action. The space-age technology and master jeweler's workmanship that went into its construction is no defense against thirty feet of saltwater, so it looks like a wrap for the camera, unless Panavision's factory can restore it. The film is something else again. A quick long-distance call to the Technicolor lab in New York and to Eastman in Rochester confirms the cameraman's instincts. The film magazine, with a 1,000 feet of film inside, is rinsed whole in fresh water, like a head of lettuce, and the entire magazine, film and all, still sealed light-tight, is totally immersed in a bucket of fresh water. The delicate emulsion will survive if wet this way, but it's got to get to the lab without dry-ing out. The lab in New York is put on red-alert standby, and Ric Fields is entrusted with the job. He rides down to the city in an airplane, cradling the bucket of water with the film magazine in it on his lap the whole way. At the airport he's met by a car that whisks him to the lab, where careful hands take the battered, wet magazine into the darkroom. In a few hours, the word comes back—the film is perfect! Not a scratch, not a bubble, not a flaw in the color! The footage is subsequently printed, the negative stored with the other neg-atives, and months later, when the sequence is edited to-gether, the shot that was taken as the *Orca* rolled into her watery grave is right in there with the other shots, and as Ollie used to say to Stanley, "And no one will be the wiser . . ."

CHAPTER FIFTEEN

"Say Good-bye to Martha's Vineyard."

(September 1974)

In a day, the *Orca* was floated by salvage divers and towed back into port, where she was swiftly repaired by crews working around the clock. By now, August was over, September had come in, and the end was in sight. The shark was behaving; the special effects department had perfected their control procedures, so it would do the same thing as often as required, and with less setup time; the cast was going quietly insane, along with their director, who could not reveal the fact. Steven would keep his cool, wait patiently for setups, work with his actors, and listen as they babbled hysterically of other projects, pictures they were missing, home and family, and Robert Shaw's income taxes.

Everyone realized the inherent cruelty of the "Indeterminate Sentence," which is California's contribution to the penal code and the philosophy of criminal correction. In California, if you're convicted of a felony, they can sentence you to "one to five years," which means a parole board will periodically review your prison record and decide if you're cool to be on the street. Originally thought of as an enlightened tool for rehabilitation, it's proved to be a debilitating psychological stress factor, since you never know how much time you have to do. If you're in there doing "ten years to life," and you're twenty years old, you could be thirty when you got out or 100—you just never know. Well, on location with *Jaws,* everyone understood the prisoners' reform movement completely. It was an indeterminate sentence instead of a fixed schedule, and it worked on people's heads.

Finally, Roy Scheider cracked. All the time he had basked on the deck, dozing in the sun, swimming off the boat, working on his perfect tan and perfectly developed body. When the weather was bad, he would huddle in the cabin with the others, making small talk, and reading *The New York Times* from cover to cover. Roy and Mike Chapman were *New York Times* junkies. They had to have their paper, and they had subscriptions and elaborate security measures taken so they could have their newspapers near them all day, ready for a fix anytime they felt faint. You could do a lot to them, but you couldn't mess with their papers. You can always spot *New York Times* junkies by the constant patting of their coat or bag, where it's stashed. They're checking to see if it's still inside, just in case someone would want to swipe the complete text of the president's message on energy conservation. In Hollywood, the poor *New York Times* addicts can be seen lining up at Schwab's Drugstore on the Sunset Strip every morning, walking over from the Chateau Marmont or the Sunset Marquis Hotel, driving down from houses with pools in the hills, looking for that crossword, the Op-Ed page, the theater reviews, the Bonwit's ads, whatever it is in all that newsprint that satisfies their craving. Chapman, who is a normally gregarious and witty conversationalist, gets downright surly and mean if his paper is swiped.[45]

Surprisingly enough, Roy's outburst was not caused by someone messing with his paper. It was a lunch that did it. Early in the filming of the ocean stuff, it was discovered that ferrying everyone into shore for a meal, then boating them all back out again took too long and was cutting into precious daylight shooting time. So the caterers took to packing box lunches every day or ferrying out mobile thermos containers of hot soup and food. The crew would find a space on the deck of the camera barge or the *Whitefoot* and eat; the director and cast would have the luxury of the *Whitefoot's* small cabin. (Built for a crew of eight, including captain and first mate, the *Whitefoot* had no room below decks for anything except the most rudimentary bunks, a tastefully appointed captain's cubicle, and a no-nonsense bridge, filled with instrumentation and controls. The rest of her was engine room and fuel.)

So here comes Roy, a mad gleam in his eyes, and he's carrying this tray of stuff that was to be lunch. Rolly Harper has to take the rap for his food all the time, and I don't know a show on the road that doesn't gripe about the chow—it goes with the territory. But this day was different from all other days, as far as Roy was concerned, and he threw the tray on the deck and screamed at the assistant director, and shouted at Steven, and then unburdened himself of all the frustrations and observations that had been bubbling inside him for the preceding months. It was probably a primal release, and it took hours for Steven to calm him down and walk it off, which isn't easy on a small boat.

Robert Shaw had his golf and his stories, Ricky Dreyfuss had his petulance and his love life; Roy Scheider finally blew it over the food and special effects delays. The cabin boy picked up the mess, and the next day Roy was fine. But the signs were clear. Everyone had been there for months—going to sea; waiting out the wind and weather, the sailboats, the crew, and the effects; suffering the separation from familiar surroundings, family, and friends. Nobody knew how long anyone else would last. We found out why, for hundreds of years, the average watch at sea is only four hours. Crews on submarines don't work the hours that movie crews work unless they're in combat, and the analogy was apt. The entire company had developed a foxhole mentality, behaving like troops in the line, experiencing battle fatigue, nervous exhaustion, and incipient alcoholism. There were more fights, more threats, and all the while the good townies of the Vineyard were stealing us blind, putting water in the gas tanks of the *Orca*, overcharging for every amenity, and behaving less hospitably every day. No one was sorry to see the summer end.

In September, it looked like a wrap. Steven, alone among all the cast and crew, had been working nonstop without leaving the island for five and a half months straight. No matter who else got sick or had the day off, the director, the camera crew, and the first assistant director are in it all day, every day. But it was soon to be over. Careful checks of the footage shot and the master script showed that the company was approaching that time when there'd be nothing left to shoot, that every scene in the script had been covered, that there was nothing to keep them on Martha's Vineyard.

Steven wanted so badly to leave, he planned an escape. He wanted no part of a drunken wrap party, no sentimental hugging and "It was a helluva show, but we did it, right?" As it was, the night before the final day's shooting, everyone was a little giddy from the reality of actually being through with the island, and over dinner at the Kelly House, Roy, Steven, Rick, Dick, David, and some others got into a furious food fight, splashing wine on each other, throwing mashed potatoes, getting a serious case of the sillies.

The next day, the last shot on the Vineyard was begun in the morning. Steven had heard that they were going to throw him over the side to celebrate, so he behaved with the fanatic caution of the obsessed. He dressed in his best leather and suede outfit, hoping that it would serve as a deterrent. ("Don't throw the kid in, you'll ruin his clothes.") He made sure to set up the shot with the cameraman the night before, so he wouldn't have to be present for the morning setup and light. When the shot was finally ready, after lunch, Steven came out to the boat. On shore, Ric Fields was waiting with a car and driver, with Steven's things all packed and ready to go. Steven checked the shot through the lens, saw that it was good, and walked quietly around the deck whispering good-byes to the New York crew (the Hollywood contingent would be reconvening in L.A. in three weeks to finish the picture). This done, Steven sprinted to the side, jumped into a waiting boat, and sped to the shore, where the car sped him to the ferry, which was scheduled to leave within minutes after they got there. Everything had been timed around the ferry schedule, and it worked. From the speedboat pulling away from the set, Steven shouted, "I shall NOT RETURN!" and then collapsed into the car for the drive to Boston. The crew finished the shot, and celebrated by throwing a few department heads into the water, as well as Cap'n Roy, skipper of the *Whitefoot,* and everybody's favorite pain-in-the-ass.

On the road to Boston, Steven started blinking and twitching, reacting to a whole new set of visual stimuli. Billboards. Traffic. Highways. Lots of cars and people. The closer the car got to Boston, the crazier he felt. It was like coming down off a five-and-a-half-month psychedelic experience, and he wasn't used to it. That night, sitting in the bar of the hotel, he and a hyperkinetic Rick Dreyfuss made a spectacle of themselves, mostly by screaming "Motherfucker, it's over! It's over! Motherfucker!" (That's Rick's influence. Steven is not so outspoken.) That night, staying in Boston to catch the morning flight to Los Angeles, Steven couldn't sleep, jolting upright in bed with a sensation of being shocked with electricity. A full anxiety attack overwhelmed him, complete with sweaty palms, tachycardia, difficulty breathing, and vomiting. When he did sleep, he dreamed he was still filming. Repetitive dreams of Martha's Vineyard kept assaulting his unconscious, and it persisted for three months after he left the island. The biggest thrill of all was getting out of the studio limousine at Universal, getting into his own car, and driving two miles back to his house. In five-and-a-half-months, he hadn't been allowed to drive a car. The pleasure of just

motoring along was the best part of being finished with location filming. For the next three months, Steven would be
troubled by dreams he kept having, that he was still on the
water, still at sea, still on the *Whitefoot* or the *Orca*, or in a wet
suit on a raft or barge, still rocking to the relentless surge of
the endless ocean. Then he remembered—Steven Spielberg,
at home, sleeps on a waterbed.[46]

CHAPTER SIXTEEN

"Hello, Hollywood, and Are We Done Yet?"

(October 1974–April 1975)

Despite the three-week "vacation" while forces regrouped in Los Angeles, the picture wasn't over yet. Bruce and his machinery had been trucked back across country, as had all the studio trucks and equipment, and there were two sequences left to complete: the discovery of Ben Gardner's boat at night and Hooper's final underwater confrontation with the monster. Richard Dreyfuss figured prominently in each, and he was increasingly antsy about the picture's protracted schedule. *Duddy Kravitz* was breaking nationally, and he was in demand for other roles; *Jaws* kept interfering with his life. But he faithfully learned to scuba dive underwater, and a stunt double his size was located who could do the complicated action and swimming required by the script. (Eons ago, when Carl Rizzo, the midget jockey, was hired to impersonate Hooper underwater, nobody knew that the "real" Hooper would be played by Dreyfuss, who is of less than average height and will hate me for revealing it. But he is short.)

Alternatives were studied, and it was decided to shoot underwater in several locations: in the waters of the Pacific off Catalina, and in one or two studio tanks, where lighting and support could be carefully controlled and where the company would no longer be at the mercy of wind and weather. The production department was ecstatic. For the first time, we'd be shooting in something like a comfortable situation, actually on the studio premises. The onset of New England autumn and winter was no longer hanging over our heads, local saboteurs were 3,000 miles away, and the crew had accumulated months of experience in controlling Bruce and making him behave on cue.

The old MGM tank built for the Esther Williams spectaculars was still available, so it was rented. The shark and its operators made their way back from the Vineyard overland, so there was some time to catch breath, look at finished film, and begin plans for postproduction. An additional underwater cameraman was engaged, a big, good-natured pro named Rex Metz. He and his crew and the short stunt double began getting underwater stuff in the Pacific Ocean, off Santa Catalina Island. Without shark platforms to worry about, the work went smoothly. Roy Scheider flew out from New York, after getting reacquainted with his family, and we all met on a dark night on the Universal back lot, where a lake was being covered in mist to simulate a fog at sea. Steven and I had agreed that the discovery of the wrecked boat would play better at night, for its spooky effect and for the tension that would build towards the moment when the staring corpse head of the dead fisherman would bump into the shot, scaring the oceanographer and the audience.

The dead fisherman was lovingly referred to as "Old Ben," or "Ben Gardner." That was the character's name, and he had been played for us by a legendary Martha's Vineyard local, a crusty, salty, blaspheming curmudgeon named Craig Kingsbury, a gentleman who qualifies for the "Most Unforgettable Character I've Ever Met" scrapbook.[47]

Craig was a rich kid from New Jersey, and he was just a young squirt in prep school when he went over the fence, took the train to Philadelphia, bought some trick dice in a magic store, and returned to school in time to wipe out the whole dorm in a crooked crap game. He won $85, and with that as his stake, he ran away to sea. That was back in the 1920s, and he's been a seaman ever since—a swordfisherman, doryman, every damn thing on the water. His dialogue was so colorful that we sent someone down just to talk to him with a tape recorder. The Kingsbury tapes later became research for the character of Quint, and a lot of Robert Shaw's colorful phraseology was inspired by Craig Kingsbury's reminiscences of a life spent at sea and his own experiences killing sharks.

Craig can be seen in the film greeting Rick Dreyfuss on his first entrance and commenting on the loony armada as it sets out to sea to catch the shark for a bounty. It was Craig who watched the confusion as we tried to set up the dock scene early in May. He looked at it all and said to Roy, "With all this damn foolishness going on, it's no wonder those directors and Hollywood people are always going bats." Had we only listened.

Craig posed for a life-mould of his head, and the makeup artists at Universal sculpted a lifelike latex bust from it, which they proceeded to distort with the grimace of sudden, violent death. It makes a great moment in the movie,[48] and I hope Craig enjoys scaring the pants off the audience. It's his face on the screen, and his character talking, in part, through Robert Shaw. Craig Kingsbury is the only man ever arrested for drunk-driving a team of oxen in Martha's Vineyard, but you'll have to get the story from him. He's a selectman in West Tisbury, and you can spot him anywhere because he's six foot three, about 240 pounds, and never wears shoes. The young folks on the island especially like him. He's always been a rebel, and I thank him just for being there.

With the last shots out of the way, the film was ready for its final assembly. The first act had been honed down almost to a fine cut, since Verna had all this time while the last act was being shot. But the last act had been saved for finishing at home, and the KEM was installed in the pool house in Verna's backyard. Steel film racks lined all the available walls, and editing tables, rewinds, and a spare Moviola or two took up the rest of the space. With Steven visiting every day, Verna continued cutting. The last act was in editorial disarray: slates listing scenes were confused or wrong, shots were included that weren't in the script, and a whole structure that had been conceived and executed in Steven's head now had to be edited into a cohesive whole. Verna's first step was to go through every shot to determine a rough continuity. "This barrel popping out of the water, which we shot in July, comes right after the boat turn, which we shot in September." Then every printed take was strung together in approximate order. ("Prints" are the "good" takes, which are saved and made into a movie. The bad stuff, the false starts, the errors, aren't even printed unless there's a pressing need for some moment that's not in the chosen take of the scene.) Most films are shot out of continuity, but individual scenes—waking up, dinner, spotting the shark, panic at the beach—are usually shot at the same time, for convenience and sanity's sake. But at sea, shots made months apart would have to be spliced together to look as if they had happened in real-time continuity.

When Verna had established the order of the last act to her satisfaction, she called in Steven, who would point out correct sequences wherever she had missed. Then they went through all the takes, organized the right take for each sequence, and Verna began the fine cut. Making the elaborate special effects work on the screen was no end of fun, and Verna admits she was never bored on this picture. Bill Caruth, who did the traditional dirty work of the assistant editor, might have been bored, but he tirelessly performed the drudgery of finding trims and scraps of outtakes, keeping it all coded and filed, and only occasionally complained about his marriage, which had been sorely tested during the extended shooting. Verna's son, Ric, no longer "assistant to the director," was "apprentice editor" again and was kept busy running back and forth to the lab and the studio—until the clutch on his car gave out. Everybody involved in the editing spent the next months locked in Verna's guesthouse, in a happy joint collaboration far removed from the pressures of location shooting. Finally, the complex physical action of the last act cut together smoothly and without fuss.

The traditional studio place for an editor is in a cutting room somewhere in the editorial building, divorced from the ongoing creative process of making the film, dealing only with the 35-mm reality of the reels of film delivered daily from the lab. But Verna had been there with us all the way, sharing meals with Steven, discovering the intent of the footage he was shooting, contributing to the very construction of the story, in cinematic terms. It was a very happy collaboration, and I believe Verna's been offered an executive creative consultancy with Universal Studios, a position difficult to achieve, much less define, and doubly rare for a woman in the industry. Once again, Universal demonstrates that as an institution, it's no dummy, and that it recognizes talent.

Christmas 1974 came and went. The original plans for the project had included a fantasy schedule that called for *Jaws* to shoot from April to June, edit until the fall, then test and preview, giving the studio the option of going for an earlier big-time Christmas release. We had only finished location shooting on September 15, and there had been three weeks more in and around Los Angeles, spaced over the next months, in which every last underwater shot and insert had been completed.[49]

Little things that would make the picture work better were picked up or reshot, and pretty soon it was all cut into place on the work print. All told, more than 400,000 feet of film had been exposed, of which 11,000 would be released as the movie, and the rest scrapped as N.G., outtake, or trim.

There were a couple of miles of technical errors alone: long shots of an empty horizon with a shark lunging up out of the water all wrinkled and showing mechanical bracing. That would be followed by an equally long shot of empty water, in which you might see the tip of a fin bubbling along. Boats that didn't sink, boats that sank too quickly, sharks that lay like a lox, sharks that shook with palsy. Actors saying lines backward, inside-out, and not at all. Extras looking at the camera. Every error, every frustration, every agonizing adrenalin surge of repressed rage, it's all got a visual counterpart buried somewhere in the unused footage.

Finally, the picture was ready for scoring and looping and dubbing. So far, no one had seen it except Sid Sheinberg, the president of MCA/Universal, who liked it, and the producers, who also were inclined to appreciate it. Besides Steven and Verna, they were the only privileged eyes. With the same iron control that he had exercised during the editing period, Steven resisted showing a foot of cut film to anyone. There was too much at stake to create a false impression with unfinished work, and despite everyone's assurances, there are precious few people, even in the industry, who can look at a work print and see what the finished release version will be like. The work print has no music, no sound effects, sometimes missing dialogue, no optical effects. It's just pieces of film taped together to run through a machine and look like a movie, it's not The Movie itself. The time had come to make *Jaws* into A Movie.

There are several stages to this. On the purely technical level, labs are prepared for timing and color-correcting the picture (they go through it scene by scene, and program printing machines to make the right light changes, so that all the blues and reds and flesh tones and backgrounds are consistent; so that scenes that are too light and too dark will be just right, so that it will look like night, or noon, or whenever it's supposed to be). The sound department begins assembling little bits of tape that include all the sound effects that are not yet on the track, from car doors and telephones through shark jaws crunching bone and flesh. This job falls to the sound cutters, and at Universal, they were a weary bunch. *Earthquake* and *Hindenburg* had been keeping them on overtime, with the new "Sensurround" multitrack process used on *Earthquake* requiring special attention and new approaches to traditional problems.

Jaws had its share of special sounds and effects, especially since the normal operating sound of the shark in the water was a continual hiss and roar of pneumatic hoses and off-camera cursing by a harried crew, with occasional exclamations from the director—"Not now, damn it. Cue the shark when he crosses into the shot, not when he leaves it." "OK, cue Bruce. C'mon—atta baby. Beautiful. Print it." All this was lifted, and replaced with baleful, malevolent, monster shark noises, specially created for the picture. (There are no existing tracks of great white sharks around, so we had to invent a vocabulary and a vocal tone for Bruce.)

Sound cutters John Stacey and Jim Troutman worked for weeks assembling reels of effects, matched synchronously to the picture. A pipe-smoking gentleman named Bob Hoyt would then "mix" the multiple tracks into a single soundtrack for the film, meshing dialogue, music, sounds, crowds, background noise, and all the complicated audio onto a single track that would then be married to the picture in a consummation devoutly to be wished. At times there would be fifteen tracks or more in the mix. Naturally, Steven and Verna were there to supervise the process, every day, every night, for every reel.

On the artistic side, a composer is engaged to write the score. Steven and John Williams had a close rapport; John's name had come up even back on the Vineyard when we had been shooting, and he was the first person to see the work print outside of the studio-executive level. He liked it and immediately got into deep discussions with Steven as they discussed how the music should be approached. They agreed that it was a film of high adventure, and Johnny went to the classic movie scores of the past for a closer listen, with Steven playing Stravinsky and Vaughn Williams albums in his office every day, looking for analogies to what he felt should be the themes. John, in the meanwhile, worked out a dramatic four-note motif for the shark, and developed themes and motifs in a manner that is sorely missing from contemporary film scoring. John had scored *Sugarland Express* for Steven, as well as such films as *The Reivers, Towering Inferno, Paper Chase, Cinderella Liberty,* and *Images,* for Robert Altman, so his capabilities were a known factor. In the liner notes to the soundtrack album, Steven commented that "the music fulfilled a vision we all shared."

When it came time to score the film, it had to be done on a certain stage within certain time limits, and Universal's studios weren't available, so a big soundstage at Twentieth Century Fox was rented. Richard Zanuck, attending the scoring, snuck on the lot and hid in the shadows, laughing to himself. A few years earlier, he had been fired from this studio in a power play reminiscent of a bad movie, his office emptied and his name painted out of his parking space before sundown. He hadn't set foot on the lot since then and had won a big contract settlement without ever passing through the gates again. The *Jaws* scoring session was the first time he had been on the lot since he had been barred from it. In the interim he had made *The Sting* with David for Universal and could afford to laugh.

At the same time as John Williams was writing his score, I sat down in Verna's little pool house in front of the KEM editing machine and began looking at the picture reel by reel, writing little bits and pieces of dialogue for "looping." Looping is the process by which actors come in after the fact and, by matching their voices to lip movements on the screen, re-create original dialogue that was unusable for one reason or another (unacceptable level of background noise, incorrect pronunciation of a word, flaw in original recording, whatever). There are a number of crowd scenes in the picture, and we had to create plausible murmuring to fill the space where all those mouths on-screen were moving.[50] In addition, there had been big cuts in a couple of dialogue scenes, and the spirit or meaning of the scene had to be compressed into a few new words of dialogue to be played while the actor's head was back to camera, so you couldn't see the disparity between what his lips were saying and what you would be hearing in the final print. (I'm giving away a lot of movie magic here, but be assured that every feature you've ever seen has been made this way, and if it hasn't bothered you before, it shouldn't bother you now. Know it, and forget you know it when you see it—that's my advice.)[51] This was my first look at the work print in continuity, although I had seen most of it in the editing process. The first time the shark comes up out of the water, I jumped in my chair. All alone in an editing room, watching it on a small screen, hearing the noise of the machinery on the track, I still jumped, and I began to believe we had something here. In the lab, the timers jumped. In the sound department, the effects cutters jumped. People always jump there, and I've seen the picture in previews with 1,200 people in the audience jumping.

The tedious process of looping the picture was over in a couple of weeks, the score was recorded, and now every element was ready to be married onto one strip of film—the "first answer print." That's a big deal in filmmaking, and it's so important it even has its own place in motion picture contracts. The film is considered complete upon delivery of the first answer print, and from then on it becomes a different kind of property. It marks the point where the director has just about completed his work. There is an important next stage, but that's nothing compared to the making of the picture. *Jaws* was about to leave our hands and go into the studio's, where it would become a "property" again and be prepared for distribution and exhibition.

Following the first answer print, a sneak preview was scheduled in Dallas on March 26. It was to be far from Hollywood so professional preview-sitters and industry wise guys would not weight the audience. Everyone wanted to see how it played in front of an audience of paying customers. The first showing is fraught with tension and high drama. Strong producers pace anxiously, palms sweat, hearts beat fast. It's like opening night of a play, and it's the first real indication of what kind of entertainment has been fashioned.

Jaws had doubled its shooting schedule and doubled its budget;[52] for $7 million invested, everyone wanted to see more than a polite murmur and a smattering of applause. Steven, Dick, David, Verna, Sid Sheinberg, and one or two others flew to Dallas, where *Jaws* would play with *Towering Inferno.*

The sneak preview had been advertised locally, and there was a line of people around the block waiting to see it. The ads had hinted at what the sneak preview was going to be, mentioning a "best-seller," and including a picture of a shark and a swimmer, cribbed from the cover of the paperback edition. People who had read *Jaws* were there in force, and we would have to face the reactions of everyone who was expecting to see the novel on the screen. The original story had been cut, revised, and changed; major characters behaved differently, and people survived who died in the book. Not only did we have to face an audience with a new picture, we also had to face hundreds of people who had their own idea of what *Jaws* was all about.

The first show was dynamite, boffo, exciting. The audience screamed and cheered, applauding and laughing, doing everything that you pray an audience will do. They filled out preview cards, handed out by ushers, eliciting their comments on what they had just seen. Prepaid mail-in cards were also provided, and for the next three weeks, they would keep coming into the studio, filled with extravagant praise, written in the privacy of people's homes, long after the initial hysteria of the group experience had worn off.

To everyone's surprise (except mine, I smugly add), there were a lot of big laughs in the picture, most of them where we had hoped they'd be. Laughs are like shrieks—hard to film, hard to edit, hard to get from an audience. That they were there was a blessing. We had always known it was an adventure picture. Now we knew it had human appeal and characters as well. Whoopee! The audience spilled out into the street; the line had grown in the meantime, and a second, unscheduled showing was added to accommodate the overflow crowd.

Back in Los Angeles, Steven and Verna trimmed places where the audience told them it was slow (referring to a cassette of the audience reaction that Verna had made, that they could use to refresh their memory of how the audience really behaved).

The fine mix that had been made of the soundtrack elements had to be changed, the acoustics of a theater being different from those of a dubbing room; some dialogue was getting lost, some effects were drowning out music. Another preview was set in Long Beach, at a shopping center theater, on March 28, two days after Dallas. Here it was to play with *Young Frankenstein*, and there was no picture of the shark in the ads, just a "Sneak Preview" ad with no hints as to what it might be. It was an hour's drive from Hollywood, again to discourage industry types from attending. This preview was another success. The lobby was filled with a happily buzzing crowd, and there was a lot of handshaking and congratulations.[53]

In the weeks to come, the picture would start getting "Exhibitor Screenings," which are like sneak previews, only with about two or three hundred theater owners invited to see the picture they will be asked to bid on in front of an audience. Exhibitor screenings were scheduled all over the country, and in New York, it was the first chance that Rick and Roy and Peter had to see their work. The New York preview was the same as the others, with an enthusiastic audience responding vociferously.

Ricky, who had been bad-mouthing the picture in the press and on interviews, was a changed man. I spoke to him at 4 A.M., New York time, and he was in a roomful of excited people, all of them still high from the movie. He and Roy had been mobbed and applauded on the sidewalk in front of the theater following the show, and as an actor, I can appreciate Ricky's newfound enthusiasm for the project. There's nothing like an adoring mob to convince you that you're OK. Rick would no longer talk down the picture, although he might take a few swipes at Universal.

By April 1975, the rumors were out around Hollywood that the picture felt good, that it seemed to be playing well for audiences. This book was commissioned, researched, and written in a very short time. After a year working on the film, during which no one had kept a journal, I had to assemble the collective impressions of dozens of key personnel, collate them with my own memory, and spin this out into a readable manuscript. I checked the preview cards one last time—were people who had read the book unhappy with the picture? Overwhelmingly, no. The changes were fine. I felt better about that. Dick and David had gone out on the personal appearance circuit to promote the paperback, at one time hitting three cities in one day, appearing on a morning show in Houston, an afternoon show in St. Louis, and a late-night phone-in radio show in Seattle. Their diligence and energy on behalf of the project paid off, and everywhere they went, they asked, curiously and nervously, if readers of the book would object to major changes in the motion picture. No, no, and no. Everyone began to breathe easier.

Any collaborative art succeeds by virtue of the positive contributions made by all the participants. Wittingly or not, the successful end product reflects the hands of dozens of artists and craftsmen. Movies, for all their size and complexity, are big celluloid mosaics—editors, actors, painters, cameramen, writers, producers, a director, all of us can point at the finished picture and pick out bits and pieces of our individual work. However, in the final presentation on the lighted screen in the darkened theater, all that personal endeavor becomes a singular parade of an infinity of still-life frames, given life and movement as a result of a perceptual process unique to the human animal and rooted in optical illusion. In the order dictated by their art, their lawyers, their agents, and their unions, the collective contributors to *Jaws* are summarized here. If you enjoy the picture, if you laugh or scream, or jump in your seat, all of us thank you. If, in addition, you've paid cash for your ticket, the producers and studios especially thank you. All of us, and hundreds more un-named, made *Jaws*.[54]

Credits

UNIVERSAL
AN MCA COMPANY
A Zanuck/Brown Production
JAWS

Cast of Characters

Brody	ROY SCHEIDER
Quint	ROBERT SHAW
Hooper	RICHARD DREYFUSS
Ellen Brody	LORRAINE GARY
Vaughn	MURRAY HAMILTON
Meadows	CARL GOTTLIEB
Hendricks	JEFFREY C. KRAMER
Chrissie	SUSAN BACKLINIE
Cassidy	JONATHAN FILLEY
Estuary Victim	TED GROSSMAN
Michael Brody	CHRIS REBELLO
Sean Brody	JAY MELLO
Mrs. Kintner	LEE FIERRO
Alex Kintner	JEFFREY VOORHEES
Ben Gardner	CRAIG KINGSBURY
Medical Examiner	DR. ROBERT NEVIN
Interviewer	PETER BENCHLEY

Directed by
STEVEN SPIELBERG

Produced by
RICHARD D. ZANUCK and DAVID BROWN

Screenplay by
PETER BENCHLEY and CARL GOTTLIEB
Based upon the novel by PETER BENCHLEY

Director of Photography
BILL BUTLER
Film Editor
VERNA FIELDS

Music by
JOHN WILLIAMS

Production Executive
WILLIAM S. GILMORE, JR.

Production Designer
JOSEPH ALVES, JR

Special Effects
ROBERT A. MATTEY

Live Shark Footage
filmed by RON and VALERIE TAYLOR

Underwater Photography	REXFORD METZ
	MICHAEL DUGGAN
Camera Operator	MICHAEL CHAPMAN
Camera Assistant	JIM CONTNER
Second Camera Assistant	PETER SALEM

Sound	JOHN R. CARTER
	ROBERT HOYT
Unit Production Manager	JIM FARGO
First Assistant Director	TOM JOYNER
Second Assistant Director	BARBARA BASS
Trainee	ANDY STONE
Script Supervisor	CHARLSIE BRYANT
Location Casting	SHARI RHODES
Set Decorations	JOHN M. DWYER
Technical Adviser	MANFRED ZENDAR
Unit Publicist	AL EBNER
Still Man	LEWIS GOLDMAN
Makeup	DEL ARMSTRONG
Key Grip	GUY POZEL
Gaffer	BILL TENNEY
Property Master	FRANK NYPHONG
Men's Wardrobe	ROBERT ELLSWORTH
Women's Wardrobe	LOUISE CLARK
Hairdresser	VERNE CARUSO
Assistant Wardrobe	IRWIN ROSE
Assistant Film Editor	BILL CARRUTH
Assistant to the Director	RIC FIELDS
Cosmetics by	CINEMATIQUE
Titles and Optical Effects	UNIVERSAL TITLE

FILMED IN PANAVISION
COLOR BY TECHNICOLOR

The producers gratefully acknowledge
the cooperation of
THE NATIONAL GEOGRAPHIC SOCIETY
and
MR. L. J. V. COMPAGNO
of
THE DEPARTMENT OF BIOLOGICAL SCIENCES
STANFORD UNIVERSITY

About the Authors

CARL GOTTLIEB is an actor, director, producer, screenwriter, and author whose books include the bestseller *Long Time Gone: The Autobiography of David Crosby* (with David Crosby). In addition to the *Jaws* screenplay, which was nominated for a Golden Globe, he co-wrote *The Jerk, Jaws 2, Dr. Detroit, Which Way Is Up*, and *Caveman*, which he also directed. For television, he has written for "The Odd Couple," "All in the Family," "The Bob Newhart Show," and received an Emmy® Award for his work on "The Smothers Brothers Comedy Hour." He directed *The Absent-Minded Waiter*, a comedy short featuring Steven Martin that was nominated for an Academy Award®. He has taught screenwriting at the University of Southern California, the University of Miami, and the American Film Institute. He lives in Hollywood, California.

PETER BENCHLEY worked as a reporter for the *Washington Post*, as television critic for *Newsweek*, and as a speechwriter for President Johnson during the last two years of his administration. Benchley's first novel *Jaws* (1974), spent more than forty weeks on the *New York Times* best-sellers list, earning him praise as the most successful first novelist in history, and was the source for the popular 1975 film, directed by the Steven Spielberg. Among Benchley's other novels are *The Deep, The Island, Beast*, and *White Shark*. He also wrote two miniseries for television, *The Beast* and *Creature*. He is currently concerned with marine conversation issues and is passionate about all undersea life, including sharks.

Endnotes

Chapter One

1. Since those innocent years, the vertical integration of the entertainment industry has led to complex relationships between studios, book publishers, television networks, newspapers, and periodicals, both foreign and domestic. The location of potential film properties has evolved into a complicated process called "tracking," and now there are even specialized independent businesses to assist in this enterprise—bookish, well-connected young people rummaging through freight-loads of new media like dope-sniffing dogs, searching for that elusive treasure known as a "marketable property."

2. For aspiring novelists, be assured this is one area where compensation is not keeping up with inflation. The numbers today for a first novel are not much better, and the chances of finding a publisher are a lot worse. And yet, the appearance of a book as an Oprah Winfrey selection increases the normal first print run of a new novel from 10,000 or 20,000 copies to 600,000, an increase in income to the author of 3,000 percent! Never underestimate the power of synergy and convergence while creating art.

Chapter Two

3. Richard Zanuck and David Brown worked together for another decade or so, making *Jaws 2*, and working with Peter Benchley again on his novel and screenplay, *The Island.* They had a number of hits, including *The Eiger Sanction*, *The Verdict*, *Cocoon* and its sequel, and *Deep Impact*. Their run ended with

Driving Miss Daisy in 1989, after which they went their separate ways, rejoining on *Rich In Love* in 1992. On his own, with his wife, Lili Fini Zanuck, and with others, Dick produced *Rush, Rules of Engagement, Mulholland Falls,* and *Planet of The Apes* (2001). He and Lili also produced the 72ⁿᵈ Annual Academy Award® Ceremonies in 2000. All continue to be active in the industry. David is now in his eighties, and still married to Helen Gurley Brown, although he's no longer writing the spicy cover blurbs for *Cosmopolitan* magazine, as he did for many years when she was its publisher.

4. Alas, no longer. Global mergers and acquisitions have made their inroads on what was once a "gentleman's trade." The German conglomerate Bertelsmann acquired Doubleday, the French La Martinière Groupe bought Harry Abrams, Inc.; many of the old-line publishers now report to corporate headquarters abroad.

5. That summer I was paid approximately $15,000 for my work on *Jaws*: $8,000 for writing, and $7,000 for acting. My wife and I bought a brand new BMW 2002 for $5,900; she picked it up to drive it to Los Angeles while I finished up on the Vineyard. When she stopped in Nashville to get the car serviced, she discovered that Robert Altman and a lot of our friends were making the movie of the same name. Allison called me, I flew down to join her and we hung out in Music City for a few days watching Altman and the crew work. Then we drove west. In Dallas, I caught a flight back to L.A. and went back to work in television. Fifteen years later I got a letter from the commonwealth of Massachusetts asking me to pay state income tax on the per diem allowance I allegedly received, which I ignored.

6. Brentano's and Walden were two early mass market book chains; they've since been swallowed up or destroyed by newer, larger mass market book chains: Borders, Barnes & Noble, and the Internet's Amazon.com. And so it goes.

Chapter Three

7. Universal Studios and MCA-Universal, independent entities! How quaint and old-fashioned that seems today. Lew Wasserman and Jules Stein sold their beloved MCA to Matsushita of Japan, who in turn sold it to Seagrams of Canada, who in turn fragmented the company and sold the pieces to the French conglomerate Vivendi. MCA-Universal was one of the last monolithic studios, but it eventually joined Warner Bros., Paramount, 20th Century-Fox, Columbia, United Artists, and MGM as subordinate divisions of global conglomerates. Say hello to Vertical Integration, and goodbye to the Good Old, Bad Old Days when Hollywood was a company town.

8. Since *Jaws*, Steven Spielberg has become one of those public figures who is universally regarded with admiration, awe, and envy. For reasons of personal security and because of his natural reticence, he's usually only seen at a distance, like a volcano or the Pope, although he's a little more accessible than the Holy Father and has a more progressive social and political agenda. Steven has an ability to make popular films that's unequalled in the history of the medium; it's no secret that he's directed many of the highest-grossing pictures of all time. Anything I can say about him is trivial, out of date, and shaded by nostalgia for the past. When we met in 1973, I was married and he was a hot young director from television with great ideas, an abiding passion for filmmaking, and an unsurpassed and obvious love for the medium. Steven was single, lived alone with two dogs, and his drug of choice was movies. We even had the same agent, Mike Medavoy, who started in the mail room at Universal, became a major talent representative, and eventually quit the agency business to be a studio chief. He ran United Artists, Orion Pictures, and now has Phoenix Pictures. Medavoy tried to make a team out of us, but we didn't sell anything because Steven was locked in to direct; studios wouldn't agree to hire him as a precon-

dition to developing our projects. He wasn't **STEVEN SPIELBERG** yet. He was just Steven. Sometimes even Steve. But that was a long, long time ago, in a galaxy far, far away. Now, I'm single and he's been married twice and has six children. We run into each other only occasionally and very briefly, usually at film industry events where we're both wearing tuxedos. We are always cordial, and he's always quite friendly.

Chapter Four

9. Joe Alves went on to design *Close Encounters* and *Jaws 2* for Steven, as well as a slew of other pictures, up to the present. In addition to being a gifted production designer, he also works as a director and has shot a lot of second unit (including *Starman* for producer Michael Douglas). In 1983 Joe Alves directed *Jaws 3-D* (the third sequel of four), on which I worked again as the rewrite guy called in at the last minute at great expense. Once again I lived alone on location with a typewriter and a series of impending deadlines, this time in Orlando, Florida, at Sea World. This time I shared screen credit with Richard Matheson, a writer for whom I have great respect, and Guerdon Trueblood, whom I've never met. Joe Alves and I discovered we have a strange connection in Dick Smothers. I wrote for the *Smothers Brothers Comedy Hour* on CBS; Joe raced Formula One cars with Dick on the race car circuit. Show business!

10. Another reference to a forgotten entity, like Brentano's. Instead of Farley Granger, read Christopher Lambert as Tarzan or anyone in *Out of Africa*.

11. How completely a quarter of a century obliterates references to barely remembered personalities of the forties and fifties. Johnny Longden was a noted jockey who still has a nice street named after him near the Santa Anita racetrack. Harry James was a famous band leader and trumpet player, and Betty Grable was an actress whose classic leggy pinup was the favorite of servicemen throughout World War II (that was the war where Tom Hanks saved Private Ryan, in Steven's movie of the same name). I have no idea who William Molter was, it's something I got from Rizzo. He was probably a trainer.

12. It's true the old special effects masters have passed from the scene, but they've been replaced by a new breed of technological wizards who work their magic using pixels and computer-generated effects. Another generation of clever technicians have supplanted candy-glass breakaway bottles and balsa-wood props with new plastics and polymers, and electro-mechanical models that blink and scream and drip gore with an explicitness that would have sent earlier audiences of horror and action films home, puking in disgust. Yet, when special effects are needed to portray a legless Vienam veteran (Gary Sinise as Captain Dan in *Forrest Gump*), the effect was achieved not only by sophisticated computer imaging but also by using a cleverly constructed wheelchair designed by magician and special effects consultant Ricky Jay's company, Deceptive Practices. They used a technology developed by stage illusionists in the nineteenth century.

13. Writer Number Two was Howard Sackler, who rose to success with his Pulitzer Prize–winning Broadway play *The Great White Hope*, which he also adapted for the screen. He also wrote *Grey Lady Down* (a naval adventure) and a film called *Saint Jack*. Although we never actually met, we also shared writing credit on *Jaws 2*, the 1978 sequel (the first of three follow-ups to the original). Once again, I rewrote his earlier draft on location during filming, this time in Fort Walton Beach, Florida. Jeannot Szwarc took over and did a fine job of directing *Jaws 2* under enormous pressure. The earlier Sackler material was the basis for Hank Searles's novelization of the movie. Howard Sackler died in 1982.

Chapter Five

14. Badlands and *Thieves Like Us* have subsequently been recognized as artistic successes, while *Sugarland Express* and Steven's TV film *Duel* are widely studied and deeply appreciated as "first features" by the most commercially successful director in the history of film. The intrinsic cinematic value of all four films is no longer an issue, and the three directors (Terry Malick, Robert Altman, and Steven Spielberg) are widely recognized as American film artists, based on the strength of these and their other works. There is some reward and respect earned by staying in the game for the long run after all, and good movies never die.

15. Again, with the hindsight of history, the budget numbers for *Jaws* have been settled with a rough consensus. The original pre-production script budget was set at $8.5 million, allowing fifty-five days of principal photography. Final budget, with overages, came to approximately $11 million, and more than 150 days of principal photography.

16. I was story editor of *The Odd Couple*, starring Tony Randall as the fastidious Felix Unger and Jack Klugman as the slovenly Oscar Madison. The series, based on Neil Simon's Broadway hit of the same title, ran on ABC from 1970 to 1975 and was developed by Garry Marshall and Jerry Belson, following on the heels of a successful 1968 film starring the late Jack Lemmon and Walter Matthau in the leads.

17. Ironically, twenty-six years later, the Screen Actors Guild contract with the Alliance of Motion Pictures and Television Producers again expires on July 1, in 2001. The Writers Guild of America contract expires two months earlier, on May 1, close to the publication date of this book. The actors already settled a bitter strike in 2000 against the producers of commercials. The issues they and the writers face as this is being written are the same: improvement of pay-for-play residuals in cable television, no rollback of existing payments on network TV, jurisdiction to bargain for Internet usage, and improved, uncapped residual payments for global replay. Once again there's a *de facto* work stoppage as studios stockpile scripts and refuse to approve production for projects that might still be shooting when the WGA and SAG contracts expire. It will be interesting to see where the unions and the industry are in 2002, much less in 2025, after another quarter of a century of evolving business models, markets, technologies, distribution patterns, and labor negotiations. In 2001, both unions settled without a strike.

Chapter Six

18. Murray Hamilton reprised his role as mayor of Amity in the first sequel, *Jaws 2.* He was one of the great character actors in the business, distinguishing himself in literally hundreds of films and television episodes. He began in the "golden age" of live television drama, appearing on *Philco Television Playhouse* and then in episodic series like *Gunsmoke, The Twilight Zone, Alfred Hitchcock Presents, The FBI, Naked City, The Untouchables,* and more. In film, he appeared in scores of potboilers and forgettable epics, as well as in memorable movies like *The Hustler, Anatomy of a Murder, Seconds, The Spirit of St. Louis,* and *Brubaker.* He was Mr. Robinson in *The Graduate.* Never a star, he was one of those reliable supporting players and co-stars who could always be counted on to supply a nuanced, thoughtful, and sensitive performance in almost any kind of drama or comedy. He died in 1986 at age 63, in North Carolina.

19. Much has been made of the politics of this casting decision, since Lorraine Gary was (and still is) married to Sid Sheinberg, which would presumably give the film and its director a little added clout in the executive suites. That's a cheap shot; Lorraine's an accomplished actress with numerous credits and in 1974 had already distinguished herself in television series. Furthermore, MCA-Universal executives were famous for putting their company's welfare ahead of any personal considerations—a legacy from the 1930s, when the parent studio, Universal Pictures, had been put into near-bankruptcy by the rampant nepotism of its founder, "Uncle" Carl Laemmle. Sid's concession to family came *after* he left MCA-Universal and went into business with his sons, Bill and Jon Sheinberg, in an independent production company called The Bubble Factory.

20. Roy Scheider, like his fellow co-stars from *Jaws*, keeps busy. He makes films and television miniseries, and has played the president of the United States more than once. That's funny, considering Roy doesn't demonstrate any of the political involvement of Richard Dreyfuss, who would rather be the president than play one on TV. Roy's a working actor in the best sense of the term; he loves the job. Like Richard and Robert, he'll never quit voluntarily. It's what he does best.

21. Similar concessions to the location's economy and politics are still being made in the modern era of "runaway" production, which in the past decade has made world film centers out of Toronto, Ontario, and Vancouver, British Columbia. A combination of tax advantages, indirect subsidies, and a weak Canadian currency makes Canadian locations irresistible to American film companies, who accommodate Canadian union demands and government quotas to get the most for their location dollars. Hundreds of "Hollywood" productions shoot in Canada every year, including many feature films. Understandably, actors, trade associations, and the unions representing the motion picture industry craftsmen and women in California and New York are enraged by the practice.

22. Richard Dreyfuss remains a friend and is still driven to distraction by his involvement with movies, television, family, and politics. Twice married, a father, and unusually fair-skinned, he continues to work unceasingly in films of distinction (and in films of not much distinction). He was born to act and was the youngest actor to ever receive an Oscar for Actor in a Leading Role, for *The Goodbye Girl* at the Fiftieth Academy Awards ceremony in 1977. He hasn't stopped since high school, where he and Rob Reiner were classmates. In addition to Dreyfuss, members of The Session included Reiner, Larry Bishop, actress-comediennes Marj Dusay and Bobbi Shaw, and David Arkin, who became despondent and committed suicide in 1990, ten years after his last acting credit. Arkin can be seen as Sergeant Volmer in the original screen version of *M*A*S*H* and in other Altman films: *Nashville*, where he reprises his hapless character as a chauffeur, and *The Long Goodbye*.

Film scholars should note that during a decade of "Bikini Beach" movies, Bobbi Shaw was Buster Keaton's last leading lady; she played opposite him in *How to Stuff a Wild Bikini* in 1965, while Marj Dusay enjoyed a long career in television and onstage. She's currently a regular on *All My Children* on ABC. Larry Bishop's father Joey Bishop was a major stand-up comedian and film actor, one of Frank Sinatra's original Rat Pack. Larry still writes and acts in action films, the most recent being *Underworld* with Denis Leary, Joe Mantegna, and Annabella Sciorra. Rob Reiner is a world-class director, one of the founding partners of Castle Rock Entertainment, and is even more involved in politics than Richard Dreyfuss. Deeply involved in universal education issues, Rob is personally identified with winning huge statewide political initiatives in California, and he continues to direct large-budget films, although he began with *This Is Spinal Tap*, now enjoying its own anniversary reissue.

23. Robert Shaw was a complicated and driven man and a lover of strong drink. He was married three times, and the father of numerous children. He complained that a simple trip to MacDonald's with his family cost two hundred dollars, which is why he kept working in whatever film roles came his way, distinguishing himself every time. After *Jaws* he made eight or ten films in four years, including another adaptation of a Peter Benchley novel, *The Deep*. (The first wet T-shirt movie, it also starred Jacqueline Bisset and Nick Nolte. Bisset wore the T-shirt.) Shaw continued to play tough guys, villains, mercenaries, and swashbuckling rogues in period adventures until 1978, when his overtaxed heart finally failed, and he died at his home in Ireland.

Chapter Seven

24. The research budget for this edition did not include a scouting trip to Martha's Vineyard. Although the exclusivity and charm of the island remain unquestioned, it has become increasingly popular with Off-Islanders, rivaling (if not exceeding) the Hamptons in Long Island as a pricey, snobbish, exclusive, vacation destination. I can't speak to the issue of fast-food franchises, but I imagine there are more of them on the island now. The Black Dog Tavern, which in 1975 was a funky hangout for local hipsters, is now an expensive restaurant that sponsors a Pro-Am windsurfing tournament, has a mail-order general store, and a Web site that advertises its T-shirts, mugs, and caps. The rising tide of tourist dollars has probably lifted the local economy to new heights and has certainly accelerated complaints among the locals and old-timers.

25. More than a few locals were employed onscreen, playing small parts. Their culture shock has been eased by the fact that twenty-five years later, they're still receiving residual checks of various sizes for their performances, even though few of them ever worked again as actors. Chris Rebello was the kid who played the older of Chief Brody's sons and was on the payroll for weeks while his scenes were shot. He calculated he made more than $100,000 in the last twenty-five years, thanks to Screen Actors Guild residual payments based on the constant revenue stream generated by *Jaws*. Jeffrey Voorhees played the luckless Alex Kintner, the kid on the beach who gets eaten by the shark; he now manages a tavern in Edgartown. His mother, played by Lee Fierro, was the woman who slaps Roy Scheider on the dock; more about her in the endnotes to chapter ten. Phil Dube played a selectman (the one who was reluctant to take his family into the water on the beach). He was a mason contractor and laid the first brick sidewalks in Edgartown, and in real life he served as selectman and assessor in Edgartown for twenty years. In semi-retirement, he held the position of building inspector for several years. He died in Florida in 2000, at the age of 90. The most notable local to work in the movie was Craig Kingsbury, 88, who's still with us as this is written, and is discussed in endnotes to chapter fifteen.

26. On the *Jaws* DVD, in the bonus materials, there's a deleted scene showing morning in the Brody household, in which Steven's dogs, Elmer and Zalman, play themselves and can be seen briefly on camera being fed by Ellen Brody (Lorraine Gary). As I recall, eating was their favorite activity, onscreen and off, followed closely by Elmer humping legs. Zalman used to bite kids, and Steven eventually gave him to Ric Fields.

27. That would be David Engelbach, who graduated from AFI and went on to a career as a screen and television writer, first with *Death Wish II* and more recently with *Blades*.

Chapter Eight

28. On the contrary, after a very brief shot at acting, Jonathan Filley realized that he could have a longer career in film if he went behind the camera. He became a location manager and followed that career track through the ranks, becoming a respected unit manager and a producer. He's steadily employed now in those capacities, working out of New York on major feature films including *The Siege, Bullets Over Broadway, Guarding Tess, Bamboozled,* and many more. Although still connected to the Vineyard, he vacations on the mainland now, closer to the city.

204 • Carl Gottlieb

29. The surface sequence in the finished film was shot on Universal's back lot, on an artificial pond that used to be known as "the Lake." The fog and lighting effects nicely mask the fact that we're no longer at sea, but only a few hundred yards from the Hollywood Freeway and Universal City, surrounded by the studio's back lot. The underwater scenes were filmed in the tank at MGM, and in Verna Fields's tiny backyard swimming pool, where Ben Gardner's head makes its final, frightening appearance. More on this in endnotes to chapter sixteen.

Chapter Nine

30. Bruce Ramer, still a powerful and influential Los Angeles attorney specializing in entertainment law.

31. It's a truism that everyone has two professions: his or her own, and show business. On the subject of popular entertainment, never have so many known so much about so little. In 1975, nobody could have predicted the modern era of accessibility, where the details of every aspect of the entertainment industry are widely publicized. What used to be the exclusive province of the industry trade press and voyeuristic tabloid journalism has crept into mainstream news. Weekend box-office grosses, budget overruns, and actors' salary demands are as likely to be featured as the latest sex or substance abuse scandal. And with vertical integration, television entertainment news shows devote a suspicious amount of programming time to the film and television releases of their parent or affiliated studios. If these programs lean towards self-promotion and sunny optimism, and fail to include any serious investigative reporting, remember that Disney owns the ABC television network, Paramount owns and distributes *Entertainment Tonight*, and the CBS News division has a family interest in seeing *Survivor* prosper. The efforts to protect the "secret" of the shark seem a quaint anachronism today, when the special and visual effects would be featured in hours of promotional material and "Making of" pseudo-documentaries.

Chapter Ten

32. Uncredited in the original film, we learn from the Internet Movie Database (www.imdb.com) that the two actors were Edward Chalmers, Jr., as Denherder and Robert Chambers as Charlie.

33. John Landis worked on this gag. At that time, he was a precocious young writer-director-star of an inventive low-budget independent comedy called *Schlock*. Landis was brought to Martha's Vineyard by producer Michael Phillips to meet with Steven on another project. "You're younger than I am," was Steven's surprised observation. Filming claimed all of Spielberg's attention, so John was left to his own devices, observing shooting when he could, accompanying Ric Fields on laundry duty, and spending time with the writer when the location was inaccessible and the towels were in the dryer. At one point while out on location, Landis was pressed into service by production manager Jim Fargo to make the breakaway pier ready for shooting, the regular lead gang being otherwise occupied. The two men spent an afternoon in the water hammering at the pier to get it right. Film historians may want to note John Landis's physical contribution to the making of *Jaws*. He soon returned to Los Angeles, where he directed the Zucker Brothers first comedy, *Kentucky Fried Movie*, and then a huge commercial success, *Animal House*, the highest grossing comedy of its time, released by Universal Studios in 1978, the same year as *Jaws 2*. He is a highly successful director and producer (*The Blues Brothers*, Michael Jackson's *Thriller* video, and many more). He's still younger than Steven.

34. This was Lee Fierro, a local talent whose dialogue was rewritten a day before her scene was filmed. A former professional actress who had left New York to raise a family in more bucolic surroundings, she objected to the profanity in the

original drafts, and Steven wanted something more suited to her Everywoman looks. After the film, she returned to the stage to the degree that she co-founded the Island Theater Workshop on Martha's Vineyard, in which she continues to be active.

35. A few weeks later, when filming the scene in which Brody and Hooper slice open the dead shark looking for the Kintner boy's remains, Richard Dreyfuss's and Roy Scheider's choked reaction to the eviscerated fish is a simple and realistic sense-memory of the awful stench on the dock that day.

Chapter Eleven

36. Verna Fields won the Academy Award in 1975 for her editing of *Jaws*. The film won three Oscars: Verna, for editing; John Williams, for his memorable score, and Robert L. Hoyt, Roger Heman, Jr., Earl Madery, and John R. Carter for sound. Verna went on to become one of the first women senior executives in Hollywood when Universal made her a vice-president with creative oversight responsibilities. She continued to nurture a generation of young filmmakers, including many women, under-represented then as now. In 1978 her supervisory duties brought her down to the set of *Jaws 2*, where in David Brown's suite, director Jeannot Szwarc and Roy Scheider got physically involved in the midst of a spirited discussion of conflicting cinematic priorities. Nothing serious, but she wound up sitting on the boys until they cooled off. Verna Fields remained a respected industry executive and sought-after voice at the studio until 1982, when cancer took her life. There are scholarships and awards in her memory at the University of Southern California's film school, once attended by George and Marcia Lucas and many of the other young filmmakers she mentored. She cannot be honored enough.

37. This Kennedy reference did not go unnoticed; after the original edition was published, I was called at home by un-named persons in the Republican camp, eager to excavate any new dirt on the Chappaquidick incident. "What was in the book is all I know," I told them, so they launched their own inquiry, which resulted in a flurry of press attention in September of 1975, the upshot of which was that, yes, the files were missing. I have no idea if they were ever returned.

38. When this book was first written, I slid right past the shooting of the *Indianapolis* scene without discussion. It seemed just one more dialogue scene in a movie that thrived on action. Since then, it's been singled out for its dark, dramatic impact, principally for Quint's memorable speech about the sinking of the *Indianapolis*, which is frequently attributed to another writer. The scene begins right after the "one barrel chase." Quint has harpooned the shark and hooked a barrel on it. There's a picturesque sunset, and we fade in later that night, in the cabin of the *Orca* after dinner. The men have been drinking. They jokingly compare scars, Hooper bears his chest and says "Mary Ellen Moffitt, she broke my heart"; Brody asks Quint about a spot on his arm where he's had a tattoo removed. "U.S.S. *Indianapolis*," Quint replies. Hooper reacts; he knows the reference. Quint then delivers a bravura monologue about the ship being torpedoed during World War II and the horror of survivors who endured shark attacks while floating for days in open water. The scene is original to the movie and doesn't occur in the Benchley novel. Howard Sackler, who was a sailor and diver as well as a writer, introduced the speech in his drafts, and we always knew it would be a big moment in the movie, "the calm before the storm." Variations of this scene are common to the action-adventure and war story genres, and in our outlines I always referred to the scar-comparing scene as "Just Before the Battle, Mother."

The "Indianapolis" speech made everyone nervous; it was two-and-a-half pages long, an immense chunk of dialogue, and absolutely essential to understanding Quint's character and obsession with sharks. Sackler worked on it. I worked on it. Steven worked on it. Steven called friends to make suggestions and write their own versions. Among the people he called was John Milius, who is often listed as having written the whole speech. Milius never denies it, and in documentaries made twenty years later, Steven takes his side. As far as I'm concerned, the author of the U.S.S. *Indianapolis* speech was Robert Shaw, a gifted writer as well as an actor.

In 1975, in anticipation of a Writer's Guild credits arbitration, I kept detailed notes and dated copies of all script materials for the entire time I was working on *Jaws.* I can recall the phone calls from Martha's Vineyard to California, and I had in my possession my handwritten transcriptions of the suggestions John made to Steven while I listened on an extension. For screenwriting trivia buffs, the complete John Milius contribution to *Jaws* is the line "I'll find him for five, I'll kill him for ten," spoken by Robert Shaw to the town meeting, shortly after Quint's first entrance. I willingly concede that the idea of a scene in which men compare scars as a macho ritual may have originated with Milius; his personal identification with manly behavior is well known and irrefutable by me.

To the best of my recollection, Shaw collated the research and examined all the drafts of the speech by Benchley, Sackler, myself, Milius, and whoever else was solicited by Steven to contribute. I can still remember the dinner at our house, early in June, 1974, when Robert joined us after dessert. He said, "I've been working on that troublesome speech," and added that he had written something he thought might work. He said he'd like to read it to us, pulled some paper from his pocket, and read, almost verbatim, the speech that appears in the movie. I knew Shaw's work as a novelist (*The Hiding Place*) and as a playwright (*The Man in the Glass Booth*), so I was better prepared for the moment, but I was as pleased and impressed by the speech and its delivery as the rest of us at the table: Steven, Dick Zanuck, Richard Dreyfuss, and

Verna Fields. There was no doubt among us that when the scene would be filmed, Robert's version of the Indianapolis speech would be the one Steven shot.

Scene 188, "Interior – Pilot House – Night" was shot on June 11 and 12, 1974. The production notes and script supervisor's lined script indicate a slow start, with the first shot taking place after lunch, after a morning of lighting, camera set-up, and rehearsal. The notes show that during the morning the scene was rehearsed, some rewrites took place, and the cast improvised some dialogue. Any work attributed to Milius of which I'm unaware could have taken place on June 11, between 8:00 A.M. and 11:00 A.M. (5:00 A.M. to 8:00 A.M. California time). After lunch, they started to shoot the scene and continued through the next day. Shaw had been drinking at lunch, and his reading of the big speech all afternoon was passionate, but not accurate. Steven was upset with him. Shaw promised to do better, and the next day read the scene cold sober. Steven then shot additional cutaways of Dreyfuss and Scheider to facilitate editing the long monologue; the version in the film is made using takes from both days, and Shaw's genius as an actor of the old school is evident; he could work drunk or sober, and still be brilliant.

Rather than have this endnote turn into a chapter, I ask only this question: Who do you believe—the guy who was there and tells you someone else wrote the speech, or a guy who wasn't there and claims he did?

Chapter Twelve

39. It wasn't quite summer when the beach scenes were filmed. Since the shark didn't work, the onshore material had to be shot at the top of the schedule, which meant May and June, when the water off Martha's Vineyard's beaches is way too cold. There was talk of rebellion from the locals employed as extras, who had to hide their coats and sweaters in their beach gear for every take and go into the frigid water for the swimming scenes. Notice there are no leaves on the trees in some of the exteriors (shot in early May). Contrary to what nit-pickers and movie blooper fanatics say on their various Web sites, almost all of the beach sequences—including Chrissie's death and the Kintner boy being eaten—were shot during the two and a half weeks between June 19 and July 6, 1974. Shoot-ing was interrupted for days at a time by a northeaster, a rainy, windy storm front that made skies gray and dismal, kept 400 extras waiting on "hold," and prolonged the schedule.

40. I don't know if Peter and Jacques-Yves Cousteau ever re-solved their differences. Cousteau died in 1997. Meanwhile, Peter Benchley wrote two more novels that were made into films, *The Deep* and *The Island.* The first was a hit; the second was less well received, although I greatly enjoyed both books. Among Peter's later works were two miniseries for television, *The Beast* and *Creature.* Although we haven't had any contact since *Jaws,* his sense of humor was still evident when we cor-responded with a British publisher who sought to reproduce a segment of our screenplay. The publisher offered an hono-rarium of $500 for publication rights guaranteed to us by the Writers Guild, to which we both belong. I said we should get $500 each, the publisher agreed, and later told me he re-ceived a wire from Peter that said "Send money immediately or all is lost!" These days, at sixty, Peter's turned his attention to marine conservation issues on a "pretty much full-time" basis. He is passionate about all undersea life, including sharks.

Chapter Thirteen

41. In the last quarter century we've seen the emergence of a handful of screenwriting gurus. Although they have sur-prisingly few actual screenwriting credits among them, they've gotten rich peddling seminars, workshops, and "how to" books that pay slavish respect to the three-act structure as the paradigm for film. A generation of would-be screenwrit-ers and development executives have taken the course and embraced the theories. Students of *Jaws*, however, will note that it's a two-act structure. The first act ends on the shot through the shark jaws in Quint's shop, of the *Orca* putting out to sea. ("One if by land, two if by sea," is a handy mnemonic device to remember which act you're in.)

42. In a contemporary photo of the shark boxed for shipment, the airplane in the background shows Federal Express markings; not quite a private charter, but not a cheapskate's choice, either, especially in those days.

43. It took sixty years for the Moviola to become obsolete. It only took a decade for the KEM and its contemporaries to be replaced by computer-assisted editing, mostly on AVID systems. In present-day editing, every frame of exposed film is transferred to multi-gigabyte hard disks as a digital image. Viewed on monitors, the images are manipulated using mouse-clicks or keystrokes rather than by physically cutting or splicing a celluloid print. The various scenes and angles can then be viewed instantly and further revised or edited. All the while, the order and sequence of manipulated images is stored in memory and on the hard drive. When a film is "locked" (i.e., editing is complete), the computer generates a list of frame numbers that correspond to the original negative, which is then conformed to the electronically edited version for making celluloid prints for distribution. The use of computer imagery makes it simple to integrate the complicated visual effects that are generated by other, specialized computers and reduces editing time taken by handling, storing, and retrieving the film's "work print." Changes can be accomplished almost instantly, and different versions can viewed side by side or in sequence, in real time. A disadvantage is that an inordinate amount of time is spent "trying things out," especially by new or inexperienced (or ignorant) directors. More importantly, the film is rarely seen projected in its true viewing size until the process is almost complete, and film projected in a theater is an entirely different esthetic experience from electronic images viewed on a monitor or even a large screen projection video. The debate continues.

Chapter Fourteen

44. The script supervisor's and editor's "lined script" was copied and presented to me in a red leatherette binding with the shark production logo on the cover; it's a treasured possession and an invaluable resource in researching this book. Lined scripts begin as a copy of the screenplay, but include dates and times of every shot made in production, notes as to exactly what action and dialogue are covered, every angle and set-up (including technical lens data), the extent of the coverage, and pertinent comments by the director. The companion document is the Daily Log Report, which is a detailed diary of every shooting day in chronological order. In it, every factor affecting production is noted: start time, time of the first shot, lunchtime, wrap time, time used for lighting, rigging, rehearsing, and shooting. Notes are kept as to wind, weather, crew health, local transportation, and any unusual events that might affect production. Present-day film people are stunned by the complete thoroughness of Charlsie Bryant's notes, which are the result of years of training in the Hollywood studio system. The need for accuracy and reliability is obvious, yet old-school studio script supervisors' practices are rarely followed today, except on the most expensive features where the most experienced personnel work. Charlsie went on to work on *Close Encounters, Black Sunday*, and a few other films. She died in 1978 after working in movies for more than twenty-five years, and she is remembered in the closing credits of Steven's comedy, *1941*, released in 1979, which says simply "For Charlsie Bryant."

Chapter Fifteen

45. Nowadays, no one has to find a newsstand, because *The New York Times* is available for home delivery in Los Angeles and many other major markets via satellite presses. Schwab's

Drugstore is long gone, torn down to make room for a multiplex cinema, a music and video megastore, a gym, a Wolfgang Puck café, and a coffeehouse, all in a huge structure that squats at the intersection where Sunset Boulevard intersects with Laurel Canyon. A block west, a strip mall paves over the site of Alla Nazimova's Garden of Allah apartments, where stars of the Thirties slept and drank and wrote screenplays. The dusty traffic island in the middle of the intersection is where the Sunset Strip Riots of 1966 started at a coffeehouse called Pandora's Box. The Chateau Marmont and the Sunset Marquis are still around, and still cool. Location, location, location.

46. Although I have no more personal knowledge of Steven's sleep habits, it's probably safe to say that he hasn't slept on a waterbed in decades; it's such a Seventies bachelor thing. However, he has been boating in these same waters recently—Jonathan Filley reports seeing Steven on a large sail yacht anchored off Martha's Vineyard in recent years.

Chapter Sixteen

47. Craig Kingsbury turned 88 in 2000, and was interviewed by *The Boston Globe* when the newspaper did a follow-up feature on *Jaws* and Martha's Vineyard. Still cranky, he's quoted as complaining, "How the hell is a shark supposed to eat someone and spit his head back into the inside of a boat?" In those days, he was also the Tisbury Shellfish Constable, and the *Cape Cod Times* reported recently that when Gertrude Kingsbury heard our company was "looking for a filthy, nasty, old foul-mouthed fisherman," she told her husband, "You have it made."

48. Audiences always reacted the same way to the sudden appearance of Ben Gardner's severed head—they jumped, physically and visibly. On more than one occasion after the film's release, Steven and my wife and I would visit the World Theater in Hollywood, where *Jaws* was playing, timing our

214 • Carl Gottlieb

visit to coincide with the moment in the film when the head was revealed. The manager would let us in, we'd stand in the back of the theater, just to watch the sold-out audience visibly rise out of their seats with a collective shriek. Whomp! I've gotten my share of laughs, both as a performer and as a writer, and Steven has moved global audiences to tears, but watching those audiences in the summer of 1975 was the most affirmative proof I've ever experienced of the power of popular art to literally move an audience.

49. The Underwater Floating Head shot has become legendary proof of the value of post-production photography: "added footage," or "re-takes" as they're called in the trade. Steven was never fully satisfied with the moment as it had been shot in the tank, but in the late stages of editing, there was neither budget nor inclination to re-shoot material that obviously worked. Frustrated by the studio's unwillingness to finance the re-shoot, Steven finally declared that he'd pay for it himself and assembled a skeleton crew, with Rex Metz as cameraman. Obliging drivers ferried the head, the boat bottom, and assorted lumber and grip equipment from storage yards on Universal's back lot to Verna Fields's house, where her diminutive backyard swimming pool would serve as an underwater location. Black plastic sheeting blocked out the sun, a gallon of milk from Verna's refrigerator was poured into the pool to give the clear, chlorinated water the look of Nantucket Sound, the boat bottom was placed, Frank Sparks, the stunt double in Richard's wet suit, went through the action, and Steven shot it until he was satisfied. The resultant footage took an ordinary shock moment to a higher level. It's a tribute to Steven's genius that he could not only imagine but also fully realize the composition and timing of a few feet of film that is forever remembered by generations of filmgoers. P.S.: The studio absorbed the cost.

50. The "looping" described here is now called "ADR," Automated Dialog Replacement, and modern technology has made an art form out of it. It was Steven's idea to use a company of improvisational actors—people I knew—to voice the crowd, so that no matter how closely you listened, or how selectively you turned up the dialog tracks, what you heard would be authentic. Prior to *Jaws*, crowd sounds were called "walla" and pulled from stock libraries or created in the sound department by casually recording a group of people murmuring "walla-walla," "rhubarb, sassafras," or some other nonsense phrase that jumbled together on a soundtrack to make a reliable non-specific crowd effect. My wife Allison and I assembled a group of improvisers who made a track that was unique to *Jaws*. A friend of Verna Fields, editor Dede Allen, was working on another Universal release, *Slap Shot*, directed by George Roy Hill and starring Paul Newman. Allen and Hill observed the "loopers" at work and used them. The effect was startlingly real, and word of mouth got to Barbra Streisand, then directing postproduction of *A Star Is Born*. She called the group to re-voice that film (I'm heard as three different people in that movie). "Looping" then evolved into a lucrative subset of postproduction sound recording, and Allison organized the loopers into the Allison Caine Group, the original, and first postproduction ADR loop group in film history. A SAG member herself, Allison took charge, recruiting and supervising improvisational actors and others with specialized language skills and voices, for postproduction recording for hundreds of feature films and television series over the next two decades. We created an annual "Looper's Ball," and "Loopy" Awards were handcrafted by Ed Begley, Jr., himself a looper and the master of ceremonies for the first event, held at our house in 1978. Within a few years, personal ambition and competitive instincts split the group. Some loopers went solo, raided accounts, and created competing groups. Others worked for whoever would hire them. Eventually it became like any other acting gig: more actors than jobs, competition for attention, and a constant scramble for employment. Welcome to Hollywood.

51. For the record, the original group of ADR actors on *Jaws* who created the modern form of looping was as follows: Carol Androsky, Dan Barrows, Allison Caine, Jim Cranna, Valerie Curtin, Murphy Dunne, Archie Hahn, Howard Hesseman, Kathryn Ish, David L. Lander, Janet MacLachlan, Michael McKean, Ira Miller, Julie Payne, Harry Shearer, Ruth Silveira, Sally Smaller, Richard Stahl, and Morgan Upton.

52. Probably $12 million "all in" at this point, not counting the expenses of releasing the picture: "prints and advertising," as the budget item is called. The entire cost of acquiring, producing, shooting, advertising, releasing, and distributing *Jaws* was far less than the P&A budget of an ordinary studio feature today.

53. The crowd's reaction was extraordinary. The most powerful corporate chiefs of MCA-Universal gathered in the men's toilet of the theater, because it was the only place in the building where you could hear yourself talk. I witnessed Lew Wasserman, president and CEO of MCA, and Sid Sheinberg, president of Universal Studios, standing on a wet tile floor with Henry H. Martin and Charles Powell, bosses of sales and distribution and publicity and promotion. Right then and there, they redesigned the release schedule for *Jaws*. Instead of the usual "platform" pattern in which a film would open in big cities and then roll out into lesser markets, *Jaws* would open wide (playing on almost 500 screens simultaneously, a huge and unprecedented number in those days). Whether they thought to maximize profits over a short period of viability, or wisely anticipated a wide national release that would earn money all summer is a moot point. *Jaws* became the first "summer blockbuster," redefined how films would be released thereafter, and established a North American distribution and marketing pattern that remains the model for the industry to the present day.

54. I'm sorry that it was not industry practice in 1975 to list all the contributors to a film in the credits. Neither the studios nor the producers kept such a roster, so it's impossible to name every person in the way that most modern films take time to do in the end credits. Where possible, I've credited people I remember in the original text and these notes. Almost everyone connected with *Jaws* in any capacity went on to have a long and successful career, regardless of his or her previous experience. Interested readers are directed to the Internet Movie Database (www.imdb.com) for a relatively complete listing of the entire cast and crew, including uncredited cast and production personnel. Every name listed can be clicked on for complete other credits. Note that while Imdb is more or less accurate in its current listings, the database is better with more recent information than it is with "historical" credits, i.e., data that did not originally exist in an electronic database and had to be manually entered.

Jaws-Related Web Sites

Some other *Jaws* links are listed below, official and unofficial. Remember, the Internet is a fluid landscape. By the time you read this, some of these may be gone, replaced by others I've missed. Most search engines will locate relevant pages with the query form "Jaws + film." Who knows what's out there!

- www.filmsite.org/jaws.html
- www.jawsmovie.com
- www.nitpickers.com/movies/titles/61695.html
- www.jaws25.com
- www.spielberg-dreamworks.com/dvd/jaws/
- www.ldm.tierranet.com/jaws.html
- www.horroruniverse.com/reviews/dvds/jaws.html
- www.jaws5.com/
- www.cinemaniacs.virtualave.net/jaws/jaws.htm
- www.ssambasivan.8m.com/jaws.html

INDEX

218

Books on Film and TV from Newmarket Press

Ask for these titles at your local bookstore, or use the coupon below.

Newmarket Insider Filmbook Series

The Jaws Log, 25th Anniv. Edition
Carl Gottlieb, with introduction by Peter Benchley
"It's like a little movie director bible." —Bryan Singer, director, *The Usual Suspects, X-Men*
___ $14.95, pb (1-55704-458-9)

Making Tootsie: *A Film Study With Dustin Hoffman and Sydney Pollack*
Susan Dworkin
"Everyone who seriously cares about movies has to read it."
—Digby Diehl
___$14.95, pb (1-55704-475-9)

Titanic and the Making of James Cameron
Paula Parisi
The only full-length narrative book on how the landmark film was made.
___$14.95, pb (1-55704-365-5)
___$24.95, hc (1-55704-364-7)

Kazan: *The Master Director Discusses His Films—Interviews With Elia Kazan*
Jeff Young
Selected as a Best Book of the Year by the *Los Angeles Times*.
___$19.95, pb (1-55704-446-5)
___$32.95, hc (1-55704-338-8)

Wake Me When It's Funny:
How to Break Into Show Business and Stay There
Garry Marshall with Lori Marshall, foreword by Penny Marshall
Memoir and show-business primer from one of film and TV's most successful writer/producer/director/actors.
___$14.95, pb (1-55704-288-8)

Newmarket Pictorial Moviebook Series

Gladiator:
The Making of the Ridley Scott Epic
Ridley Scott
5 Academy Awards, including Best Picture and Best Actor
___$22.95, pb (1-55704-431-7)
___$32.95, hc (1-55704-428-7)

Crouching Tiger, Hidden Dragon:
A Portrait of the Ang Lee Film
Ang Lee, James Schamus
4 Academy Awards, including Best Foreign Language Film
___$19.95, pb (1-55704-457-0)
___$32.95, hc (1-55704-459-7)

Planet of the Apes:
Re-Imagined by Tim Burton
Tim Burton, Mark Salisbury
___$22.95, pb (1-55704-486-4)
___$32.95, hc (1-55704-487-2)

Newmarket Shooting Script® Series

Traffic: *The Shooting Script*
Stephen Gaghan, Steven Soderbergh
Academy Award Winner:
Best Adapted Screenplay
___$18.95, pb (1-55704-778-3)
___$24.95, hc (1-55704-482-1)

Cast Away: *The Shooting Script*
William Broyles, Jr.
___$17.95, pb (1-55704-481-3)

American Beauty:
The Shooting Script
Alan Ball, Sam Mendes
Academy Award Winner:
Best Adapted Screenplay
___$16.95, pb (1-55704-404-X)
___$22.95, hc (1-55704-423-6)

The Shawshank Redemption:
The Shooting Script
Frank Darabont, Stephen King
Academy Award Winner:
Best Adapted Screenplay
___$16.95, pb (1-55704-246-2)

The Frasier Scripts
David Angell, Peter Casey, David Lee
"Translates superbly to book form."—*Entertainment Weekly*
___$18.95, pb (1-55704-403-1)